Publishing Notice

G000162589

Naming, mentioning or referencing any organisation (including companies and authorities) in this book does not imply that they are endorsed by the publisher or author. Neither the publisher nor the author have been endorsed by any organisation (including companies and authorities) mentioned in this book.

Contact details mentioned in this book (including addresses, phone numbers, web-sites, internet addresses and email addresses) were correct at the time of publication. Contact details may change and then not be updated in this book.

'Ironman' is a registered trademark of World Triathlon Corporation (WTC). Official Ironman Races involve the recognised iron-distances (swim 2.4 miles, cycle 112 miles and run 26.2 miles). Iron-distance races that are not organised by WTC must not be called "Ironman".

CONTENTS

Section A - "On Your Marks"

Section B - "Get Set"

Section C - "Go"

Section D - "Finish"

Section E - "Kona"

Dedication

This book is dedicated to Bill Capps, who had Alzheimer's Disease.

In addition, this book is dedicated to Annette and the other people who cared for Bill.

Bill was an Oxford Graduate and former Rotary Club President.

Bill devoted his life to public service and charitable works.

I am proud to be Bill's son-in-law.

Introduction

Is this your first marathon or do you want to run marathons faster than ever before?

Either way, you've come to right the place!

My first marathon finish was 4:46 in 2008, aged 45.

At age 53, I am getting faster than ever with a 2:51 finish in 2016. Furthermore, that lifetime best time was the middle race of 3 marathons run in 3 weeks with each one finished under 3 hours.

This book will guide you through systematic time-efficient methods that can make you fitter, faster and more resilient. The secrets to success are revealed within the pages of this book, so please don't tell any of my age-group rivals about these things.

The advice and methods documented in this book are based upon my knowledge accumulated by studying the sport and personally racing more than 50 marathons (plus 20 iron-distance triathlons, an ultra-marathon and 1 double-iron-distance triathlon).

My medical background does provide some important perspectives, but this is not a medical book. Ask permission from your own physician (doctor) before using my methods.

This book contains detailed (mile-by-mile) Marathon Race Plans and detailed 12 to 16 week Training Plans for runners aged from 18 years to 75 years and for Marathon Finish Times from 2:14 to 6:14.

The 12 to 16 week Training Plans cater for all levels of ability. The easiest Training Plan starts with just 11 miles running each week and has a Peak Training week of 24 miles. The Hardest Training Plan has Peak Training of 100 miles weekly.

This comprehensive guide includes advice about nutrition, lifestyle, injuries and ailments. Train smart in order to get impressive results safely and enjoyably.

The aerobic and anaerobic energy releasing systems of the body are explained. This is not rocket science. Do the right things and your body will make the right changes.

Your marathon journey is going to be amazing. It is a privilege for me to be involved.

Best wishes. Dr Jim.

Health Warning and Disclaimer

<u>In general, running is healthy and good for people.</u> However, like many things in life there are associated hazards and risks.

Far more potential harm comes from inactivity and lack of exercise than potentially comes from running. There is currently an epidemic of obesity and psychological disorders that can in many cases be remedied by the lifestyle promoted within this book.

This is a reference book for runners and triathletes. Though it is written by a doctor of medicine, it is not a medical book.

Information in this book is intended to guide you to make your own decisions about lifestyle, nutrition, training and racing. This book is no substitute for you consulting with health professionals or fitness professionals.

Hopefully, this book will be read (and the plans adopted) by all kinds of people with varied health status and fitness levels. Most people should be encouraged to take up running even if they have health problems.

The key to successful and safe running is GRADUAL ADAPTATION.

This book (and the lifestyle it promotes) should be used to gradually make changes for your body and mind. Neither non-runners nor experienced runners should try to do too much too soon.

If you have a health condition that might be worsened by running, please do consult your physician before attempting any of the training or lifestyle changes mentioned in this book.

Disorders of the cardiovascular system are clearly a concern for activities that require the heart rate to rise, so please consult your physician before doing the things mentioned in this book.

People with disorders that alter consciousness (such as epilepsy, insulin-dependent diabetes and syncope) should consult their physician (doctor) before doing the things mentioned in this book.

Question: Does Dr Jim advise that people who are known to have health problems should ask their physician (doctor) to give them permission to attempt marathon running or follow the advice, plans, schedules, diets, activities in this book?
Answer: Yes. Definitely. As you have known health issues, you must seek medical advice.

Question: Does Dr Jim advise that people who are <u>not</u> known to have health problems should ask their physician (doctor) to give them permission to train for a marathon?

Answer: Yes.

Question: Does Dr Jim advise that people who are <u>not</u> known to have health problems should ask their physician (doctor) to give them permission to follow the advice, plans, schedules, diets, activities in this book?

Answer: Yes. As with all exercise plans, you should seek medical approval before you start.

Question: Did Dr Jim (or many of his many friends who have run marathons) ask their own physician (doctor) for permission to train for a marathon?

Answer: No. Maybe we were foolish. However, fatalities from marathon running are very rare, considering the huge number of people who participate in marathons. This is not a dangerous activity compared to many other things we do in life.

Heart Rate Disclaimer

Training to run fast marathons does inevitably require the heart rate to rise very substantially at certain times.

If your heart is not accustomed to having a heart rate near to the estimated maximum for your age (eHRmax), there will be some risks associated with trying to make your heart do things that it cannot do safely.

Therefore, you should not attempt very high heart rate activities such as those mentioned in the race plans and training plans in this book.

If your body is already adapted to regular exercise and you know your maximum heart rate (HRmax) from training or racing with a heart rate monitor (HRM), then risks from high heart rate activity should be minimal.

Section A

"On Your Marks"

CHAPTER 1

Gradual Adaptation

A city isn't built in just one day

Our bodies and minds are extremely adaptable. Far more adaptable than most people realise. Many people are disheartened and de-motivated by setbacks. Some people overcome setbacks with ingenuity, patience, determination and even stubbornness. We all know people within this second group and we should draw inspiration from them. Examples of inspirational people are celebrated later in this book.

The setbacks that people have overcome (in order to participate in sport or other activities) can be huge. These setbacks include illness and disability as well as many other things.

Adaptations do not occur overnight and we must be patient. Nevertheless beneficial changes do start within days of a stimulus. Different types of training stimulates our bodies to respond in numerous different ways and an appropriate mix of various mental and physical exercises will maximise beneficial effects.

Just running at the same pace and for a similar distance every training session will not produce many gains. We need to force our bodies (in a good way) to make changes by challenging ourselves.

Multi-sports (such as triathlon) are a proven way to add variety to a runner's training. Such variety adds to the enjoyment and increases the volume of training that is possible before over-use injury occurs. Mostly runners get over-use injuries affecting their lower limbs. Swimming and cycling tend to make runners more resilient to injury as well as improving cardiovascular fitness.

Swimming and cycling are essentially non-weight-bearing activities that tone-up muscles in a more gentle way than running does.

In order to consolidate and build up these improvements we need to regularly repeat the stimulus that creates them. Sadly, these gains do rapidly slip away back to our baseline level when we neglect our training or do not have a healthy lifestyle. In its extreme case, lack of exercise and poor lifestyle makes people 'de-conditioned'.

Sadly, lack of fitness is becoming the norm as a result of typical modern diets and behaviours. Much preventable morbidity and mortality occurs as a result of unhealthy lifestyle, but that is not within the scope of this book.

Changes in exercise routines must be gradual and incremental to maximise benefits. If it is not sufficiently gradual then injury is likely to occur. The body needs to be challenged but not beyond its ability to cope (given the current level of ability).

There is zero need for any illegal substances (performance enhancing drugs) to make beneficial adaptations for our bodies. Drugs cheats are fools.

CHAPTER 2

Facts, Opinion and Dogma

There is a massive amount of information out there in the world on the subjects covered by this book. A lot of that information is opinion rather than scientific fact.

As a practicing physician, I am familiar with scientific research and how to judge the quality of the various pieces of information.

At times, sport is more of an art than a science. Nevertheless it is good to be methodical and rigorous in our approach.

Understanding the principals of how our bodies function is a great help in deciding how to manage our lifestyles and training plans. It is good to be logical about which training methods to adopt and when to use them.

The strategy needs to be fundamentally simple with underlying themes that are easy to understand. We need to have sustainable enjoyable repeatable habits that become automatic and easy.

Myth-Busting

A number of my training, racing and lifestyle habits are slightly unusual. I like to think that they give me a competitive edge when it comes to racing. Different things will work for different people. Getting the body adapted to endurance sport (and adapted to using fat as the main fuel) seems to be important for many of the things mentioned in the following pages.

1. "Tapering"

It is true that runners should gradually reduce the overall volume of training during the final 3 weeks before a marathon. However the once weekly long training run should not be reduced too much. Endurance adaptations do diminish after just 10 days of the last long run.

The Training Plans in chapter 18 of this book have a sensible approach that will suit most people and often my own training follows precisely this formula. Conversely I sometimes alter the plan and do a 20 to 26 mile run within 6-14 days of a marathon race or iron-distance triathlon. This has produced some personal best times for me, so you may wish to try it yourself.

My best marathon time (2:51) came just 2 weeks after running a 2:59 marathon.

My best iron-distance triathlon run (3:26) came 6 days after running a 3:45 marathon.

Nevertheless, I do only a couple of 30 minute runs in the 7 days before a race (and rest the legs completely on the day before the race).

2. "Multiple Marathons"

It is often said that it is best to avoid too many marathons and one should leave a gap of several months between marathons. However, the more marathons that I race the faster I get.

Paris (2:59), Brighton (2:51) and London (2:55). All completed within a 22 day period in April 2016. Brighton and London (my best and third best marathon finishes ever) were 7 days apart.

3. "Carb Loading"

I increase carbohydrate intake for a couple of days before the marathon but there is no need to overdo this (if you have become properly adapted to "fat-burning").

4. "Running will give you arthritis"

The association between marathon running and arthritis is weak, in my opinion. There appears to be a stronger association between inactivity/obesity and arthritis.

I had a bad knee and a bad ankle before I became a runner. I assumed that a single marathon would destroy my joints, but regardless of this I wanted to complete just one marathon anyway. Fifty marathons later, my knee and ankle seem better than ever.

5. "Eating fat will make you fat"

I tried the traditional dieting methods to get lighter in order to run faster. These methods got me down to 10% body-fat for brief periods but this could not be sustained.

I started on the Low Carb High Fat (LCHF) diet a couple of years ago and my body-fat is now stable at around 8% but I can get it down to 5-6% for races. See chapter 5.

A close colleague at work was so impressed with the effects she saw in me, that she tried the LCHF diet for herself. Within a year she lost 50 pounds in weight (and this is still reducing). Her husband has lost 60 pounds and the pair of them are about to go skiing, because they are fitter than they have been for years (despite numerous other diets in the past).

6. "You need carbs throughout the day to maintain energy levels"

The opposite is true. Carbohydrates are rapidly digested and this energy spike has to be counteracted by an insulin surge that is followed by an energy slump. That is why constant snacking takes place on a typical Low-Fat diet.

When oil and fat make up the majority of the body's fuel intake, the energy levels are good and also steady throughout the day. Greatly reduced snacking urge occurs as a result.

7. "Athletes need a high protein intake"

A moderate protein intake is needed to re-build damaged muscles and that sort of thing. Protein must not be the main source of fuel intake for the body, otherwise the body adapts to using protein as fuel.

A body adapted to using protein as the main fuel source will 'burn muscle' for fuel when dieting or when doing long exercise sessions.

We need the body to adapt to using fat as the main fuel, so that it 'burns fat' during dieting and long exercise sessions (including marathons).

8. "Avoid Trying New Things"

Trying different things can make training more interesting. We cannot always justify buying a new piece of kit to rekindle our enthusiasm.

Sometimes we can get re-enthused by a new training technique or nutrition method. It is good to try out new things as well as having embedded routines of good habits.

It is best to not try anything new for the first time during an important race.

9. "Multiple Iron-Distance Triathlons"

The established consensus seems to be that it takes a few months to fully recover from these 8-17 hour races. My preference is to do an iron-distance triathlon once each month for the 3 months of Autumn.

Usually my second or third race of this series is my fastest. The endurance adaptations created by these races seem to give a performance boost and it is a shame not to make good use of that.

CHAPTER 3

Running Styles and Form

Figure 1.

Rio 2016: Gwen Jorgensen Won Women's Triathlon with great running form. This gold **medal** is the first for the U.S. in the event at the Olympics

Running styles vary, even amongst those of international standard. Despite this variation, there are some characteristics that do seem more efficient and the best runners usually do these things correctly.

By contrast, swimming strokes have much less scope for variation and tiny inefficiencies greatly reduce propulsion or increase drag.

Figure 2.

Kenya's Dennis Kimetto Broke the World Record at Berlin Marathon with 2:02:57 to be the first to go under 2:03.

Figure 3.

Paula Radcliffe (GBR) is the current world record holder for the women's marathon, which she set during the 2003 London Marathon, with a time of 2:15:25

Paula Radcliffe runs with some 'bobbing' head movements, that one would not necessarily want to emulate, but this appears to do her running efficiency no harm.

Paula runs with a straight vertical neck and back, which is worth emulating. Her pelvis is well forward. Her straight vertical back allows the neck to be straight (and indeed slightly bent forward).

Most runners fail to achieve Paula's perfect posture, resulting in the back bending slightly forwards so the neck is forced to bend slightly backwards (in order to see where they are going).

Consult your coach, therapist or physician (doctor) before changing your running style.

I aim to do the things below:

Posture

Good posture is easier to achieve when runners are not tired and when core body strength is good. As runners get tired, the pelvis tends to drop back and the torso tends to bend forwards then the foot strikes the ground in front of the pelvis.

When you get tired it is best to concentrate your efforts on keeping the correct posture as this maintains running efficiency.

When the neck is bent backwards, to compensate for the back bending forwards, there is increased tension in the neck muscles. This muscle tension increases fatigue.

The arms should be held relaxed with the elbow at 90 degrees. The hands should be relaxed without a tight fist.

Keep the pelvis forward with back straight and have the foot strike the ground underneath the pelvis. Run as if you were trying to make yourself look as tall as possible. The runner on the left has better posture than the other runner in Figure 4.

Figure 4.
Dave Scott (USA) and Mark Allen (USA) both smashed the previous World Ironman Record at the 1989 Ironman World Championship, in Hawaii. This day of racing will be forever known as "Iron War" and many people consider it to be the greatest Ironman race ever. At the finish line, after 8 punishing hours racing shoulder to shoulder in all 3 disciplines, both men were separated by less than a minute. In this image, Dave Scott (on the left) has superior running form, with his pelvis further forwards and his spine more vertical.

Heel striking vs. Forefoot striking

Hitting the ground with the heel first is the norm when walking even with bare feet, but heel-striking when running requires shoes as it would hurt otherwise. Presumably our early ancestors were obliged to have the front of their foot (forefoot) hit the ground first when running until shoes were invented.

Be prepared to employ both heel-strike running and forefoot running, depending on the situation. Variables include running speed, gradient (uphill or downhill) and current injury status. It is good to 'mix it up a bit' during long distance running, because this varies the stress on different joints and muscle groups so there is reduced fatigue and injury risk.

Heel striking tends to be best at slower pace (below 7-minute miles). This allows a longer stride and reduced cadence (paces per minute) plus less strain on the Achilles Tendon and calf muscle.

Forefoot running tends to be best at faster pace (above 7-minute miles). The stride is a little shorter but the cadence can be raised very high. There is less impact on ankles, knees, hips and spine because the knee is slightly bent (resulting in shock-absorption by the leg muscles and tendons).

Efficiency whilst running up and down gradients with heel striking or with forefoot striking varies between individuals but generally one finds that heel striking has a braking effect when going downhill. This braking effect should be avoided on moderate descents but it may become essential on extreme descents.

Running vs. Walking

'Power walking' up a steep hill can be as fast as, and more efficient than, running up that same hill. I often do personal challenges during races with steep hills, whereby I try to power-walk up hills faster than other people are running. This is quite fun actually. It can be refreshing to use the different muscle groups employed with 'power walking', so short periods of brisk walking at regular intervals during a marathon race is likely to delay the onset of fatigue and may result in a fast finish time.

It is important to try out all the different styles in training to see what works best for you. Trying something different does sometimes create a 'break through' and an improvement in form. Checking progress, moment by moment, with heart rate and speed monitoring is ideal in order to find out what will work best in any given situation. Test this out in training rather than doing it for the first time during and important race.

Walk:Run Strategy

In some marathon races, you may not be able to run all 26.2 miles. This may be due to set-backs in training or because it is a marathon that is part of an iron-distance triathlon. In this situation, it can be advisable to walk briskly for one minute at the end of each mile that is run.

This greatly reduces fatigue and it is a tactic that is best employed from mile 2 onwards. It is better to walk briskly for one minute every mile (a total of 25 minutes) rather than walk slowly for a whole hour at the end of the race.

The brisk walking should aim to be at the same cadence (paces per minute) as the running. This way the runner's rhythm is maintained and the speed does not drop too much during the process.

It is important to practice this in training in order to get proficient at this brisk 'power walking'. Try to emulate Olympic Marathon Walkers, who can achieve an average pace that is less than 2 minutes per mile slower than the Olympic Marathon Runners.

Aim to coincide each 60 seconds of walking with either an up-hill section or a feed-station. Do not walk down-hill because that would be wasting the opportunity to travel fast with low effort running.

CHAPTER 4

Monitoring Heart Rate and Speed

It is very important to be familiar with your heart rate and understand the significance of it. This allows more effective training and racing.

Heart rate instantly gives an accurate guide to pacing during a race and proper pacing is fundamental for long distance racing.

The relationship between heart rate and speed at any given time gives an indication of running efficiency and fitness level. This reveals progress within the training schedule and within a race.

Heart rate and speed are best monitored simultaneously with a good quality GPS (Global Positioning System) watch. These are objective measures that reveal the true levels of effort and fatigue.

Chest strap heart rate detection has in the past been the only way to get reliable data but technology improvements have recently allowed effective wrist heart rate detection from the GPS watch itself.

Slow-Twitch and Fast-Twitch Muscle Fibres

Most people are born with a fairly well balanced mixture of both slow-twitch and fast-twitch muscle fibres.

It seems that many muscle fibres can behave in either fast-twitch or slow-twitch mode. This can be influenced by training.

Slow-twitch fibres are better for endurance and fast-twitch fibres are better for sprinting.

There is a lot of potential adaptation for most of these muscle fibres. Therefore with appropriate training most people can become fairly good at either sprinting or endurance but they will never be Olympic standard in either type of racing.

It is possible for some muscle fibres to be particularly specialised and Olympic Sprinters seem to be born with an exceptionally high proportion of 'super-fast-twitch' muscle fibres, so sprinting is their destiny.

Perhaps Olympic Marathon runners tend to be born with an advantageous composition of particularly specialised slow-twitch muscle fibres. However, there are many additional factors required to achieve marathon excellence.

Aerobic vs. Anaerobic

When exercise begins, glucose derived from glycogen stored in the muscles reacts with oxygen to release energy. This is called 'aerobic' because it requires oxygen. As the glycogen stores diminish, glucose released from the liver (or absorbed from the stomach from gels and energy drinks) gets used to release energy.

If there is not enough oxygen delivered to the muscles, the energy is released from glucose without oxygen by an 'anaerobic' process.

The body has a limited ability to remove the waste products of this anaerobic process. When these waste products (mostly lactate) build-up, there is reduced running efficiency and increased fatigue causing slower running pace.

Fat metabolism rises in response to falling glycogen levels that occur during exercise. Both fat stores and glycogen stores can be used to release energy aerobically.

The following table is perhaps an over-simplification, but it is intended to summarise the characteristics and differences between aerobic and anaerobic processes (as well as muscle fibre types).

	use O2	make lactate	muscle fibre	best for	can use glucose	can use fat
aerobic	yes	no	slow-twitch	endurance	yes	yes
anaerobic	no	yes	fast-twitch	sprint	yes	no

A simplified way for marathon runners and triathletes to think of these issues is as follows:

The **aerobic** system uses oxygen and body-fat as fuel to produce power from **slow-twitch** muscle fibres. This predominantly happens at low HR (heart rate). We want to do mostly this during endurance events like marathon running.

The **anaerobic** system uses glucose as fuel without oxygen to produce power from **fast-twitch** muscle fibres. This predominantly happens at high HR. We want to do this only when we do our race sprint finish because the anaerobic system is relatively inefficient and it produces a build-up of waste products that rapidly make us feel fatigued.

For any given HR, we are using some aerobic and some anaerobic power. The lower the heart rate (HR), the greater the contribution of aerobic. The higher the HR, the greater the proportion of anaerobic.

Our bodies can clear the waste products of the anaerobic system, so long as the rate of production of waste products is within our **'lactate threshold'**. Lactate (or lactic acid) is the main waste product that makes our muscles fatigue with high HR exercise.

Heart Rate (HR) Zones

It has become established jargon to categorise HR rate into Zones. I am not sure who first invented 'heart rate zones', but there are numerous classifications quoted by different sources.

I have seen HR Zone tables with 3, 4, 5, 6 or 8 different zones. Most people I know, simply talk about Zones 1-4.

Bear in mind that this is a continuum rather than a step-ladder. Dividing heart rates into zones is a concept that has been created by researchers (and coaches) to help our understanding. One zone blends seamlessly into the adjacent zones.

My advice on HR for racing and training will be based on a classification of 'how much below maximum heart rate' is advisable for any given scenario.

Zone 1 is a low intensity relaxed pace that could be maintained practically all day and almost exclusively employs the aerobic system. HRmax-80to70 (80 to 70 bpm below maximum heart rate).

Zone 2 is what is used for a typical long training session. This level of effort can be maintained for several hours and it is less intense than race pace. HRmax-60to50.

Zone 3 is a typical race pace for endurance sport such as marathon running. HRmax-40to30.

Zone 4 is a high intensity effort that can only be maintained for short duration (a few minutes or longer depending on level of fitness) and almost exclusively employs the anaerobic system. HRmax-20to0.

<u>Do please ask permission from your physician (doctor) before attempting to raise your heart rate this high.</u>

Z1	**= HRmax - 80 to 70**
Z1-2	**= HRmax - 65**
Z2	**= HRmax - 60 to 50**
Z2-3	**= HRmax - 45**
Z3	**= HRmax - 40 to 30**
Z3-4	**= HRmax - 25**
Z4	**= HRmax - 20 to 0**

Maximum Heart Rate (HRmax)

You need to know your own HRmax as it varies a lot between individuals and HRmax is the basis for estimating the four heart rate zones (HRZ 1-4).

HRmax can be estimated (so let's call this eHRmax) with this simple formula. eHRmax = 220 - age
Examples:

(Age 20) eHRmax = 220 - 20 = 200
(Age 50) eHRmax = 220 - 50 = 170
(Age 70) eHRMax = 220 - 70 = 150

However, this estimate can be inaccurate in many individuals. I recommend that you pay close attention to your personal heart rate rate during very intense exercise in order to find your actual HRmax. Ignore some of the wild variations that may register at times when the heart rate monitor may have poor signal.

For instance I have a friend the same age as me, who runs marathons in around the same times. We are of very similar fitness levels and athletic ability. The calculations on the previous page estimate our eHRmax to be 167, whereas my actual HRmax is 180 and my friend's actual HRmax is 165.

How do we know our actual HRmax? The answer is simple. This is the heart rate that occurs during the last 100m of a 5km race or a hard sprint interval training session.

<u>Do please ask permission from your physician (doctor) before attempting to raise your heart rate this high.</u>

I do wonder whether my friend could push himself a bit harder, but he is a very competitive person who probably is giving 100% effort. The most likely explanation is that we have rather different cardiovascular systems, even though we are similar age, weight and height. Interestingly, this difference between our heart rates occurs throughout the heart rate zones. So he runs marathons with average heart rate of around 145, whereas my average is around 160 but we finish in around the same time.

Pacing

It is essential that we run at our own optimum heart rate in order to get our optimum race finish time.

If I ran with average heart rate of 145 (it would be like a training effort, so my marathon time would be around 30 minutes slower than my potential).

If my friend ran with 160 heart rate for a marathon he would fatigue within an hour and would have to complete the marathon by walking.

For 5k, 10k and half-marathon races it is best to get fully warmed up for 20 minutes before the start then go for target race pace almost straight from the gun.

For 5k and 10k races the heart rate rises to around HRmax-10to20 (10-20 beats per minute slower than maximum) within a minute or so of the gun, then this HR is maintained until the final sprint starts. When fit enough, this strategy can work for half-marathon.

Try to get to HRmax as you hit the finish line, then you will know you have tried your best.

You must ask permission from your physician (doctor) before attempting to raise your heart rate this high.

Pacing for a marathon is crucial and rather different than for shorter distance races. The warm-up may be 10-20 minutes but at gentle pace (around HRmax-50). It is important to conserve glycogen energy stores for the race and hope to have completed the first couple of miles before the anaerobic system gets triggered.

Throughout the bulk of the marathon, one uses a mixture of aerobic and anaerobic systems. Training and endurance fitness makes us better adapted to using the aerobic system, but the higher our HR rises the greater is the proportion of the anaerobic system's contribution.

During the marathon our body gradually fatigues in numerous ways and the effect of that is less with better training, fitness and form. This fatigue leads to a tendency for our speed to drop for a given HR, so to maintain our goal pace we gradually increase effort and our HR rises.

Miles 4 to 13 need approximately HRmax-30 and miles 14 to 23 need approximately HRmax-20, but the rise in HR is a gradual continuum with no sharp increases. Miles 24 to 26 will ideally see the HR gradually rise near to maximum by the finish (if we are having a good day and there is not excessive fatigue).

<u>You must ask permission from your physician (doctor) before attempting to raise your heart rate this high.</u>

It is vital not to let the HR drift up early in the race, but towards the end of the race we have less to lose. We can 'give it our all' during the last few miles as the finish line beckons.

It is best to give almost 100% effort during mile 25, because mile 26 (and the 0.2 mile right at the end) will take care of themselves. Determination and the cheers of the crowd will make us 'dig-deep' for the last bit.

There is no substitute for experience when it comes to marathon pacing. The more marathons you race, the more your mind and body adapt to managing the 26.2 miles most efficiently.

There will be good performances and poor performances, but they are all learning opportunities.

When it all goes well on the day, we need to make a 'mental file' of how wonderful it felt and what we did to make it happen.

Training with Heart Rate

Heart rate monitoring is excellent to ensure that training regimens are as effective as possible. This is because heart rate at any given time provides an accurate <u>objective</u> measure of effort level.

Another accurate objective method to measure effort would be a running power meter, but that is a relatively new technology that is not widely used currently.

<u>Subjective</u> effort level (also known as perceived effort) may be inaccurate because it is influenced by state of mind and level of fatigue.

It is important to train at specific effort levels for different training sessions and at different stages within a training session.

Training regimens can be complicated and confusing, but in essence it is simple. Low heart rate exercise is the bulk of what marathon runners need as this creates adaptations to the aerobic system and to endurance.

High heart rate exercise (sprint intervals or 5k races) are needed to build strength and to adapt the body to cope with waste products of anaerobic activity (lactate threshold).

Resting Heart Rate

This is the minimum HR. It is the HR that occurs when first awakening in the morning or when lying down totally relaxed.

The resting HR is affected by certain medications (such as beta-blockers) or medical problems (such as heart block), however, in the absence of those scenarios it helps us judge fitness level.

Generally, an average person has a resting HR of around 60-75 bpm, whereas a well trained athlete will have a resting HR between 49- 59. The figures are approximations. Female athletes tend to have HR around 5 bpm faster than male athletes on average.

Do please consult your physician (doctor) if your resting heart rate seems to be too high or too low.

Resting HR will steadily drop as fitness levels increase, so some athletes might be interested in it for that reason.

Some athletes notice that their resting HR rises when they are over-trained or exhausted, so this indicates that they should ease off training for a few days.

CHAPTER 5

Nutrition

You must consult your physician (doctor) before following my advice or changing your diet.
Patients with diabetes, heart disease, raised cholesterol or epilepsy should be particularly careful to always adhere to their own physician's instructions.

Low Carb High Fat (LCHF) is sometimes called Low Carb Healthy Fat.

I paid little attention to nutrition up until December 2014, when I read the newly published "Low Carb, High Fat Food Revolution: Advice and Recipes to Improve Your Health and Reduce Your Weight" by **Dr Andreas Eenfeldt**.

Many thanks to Jane and Malcolm at http:// www.aspirefitnesssolutions.co.uk for lending me this book and opening my eyes to the benefits of correct nutrition. Like many athletes, Malcolm has been adhering to a LCHF diet for some time and the benefits are clear to see in terms of his race times and physique. Here is Malcom's blog: http:// lchf4runners.blogspot.co.uk

Initially, I was very sceptical about any dietary advice (including LCHF). Scepticism about 'revolutionary' health solutions is a reasonable starting point for any scientifically-minded person.

Eenfeldt's book is well written and presents a body of compelling evidence (including from numerous large clinical trials). I was sufficiently convinced so I gave LCHF a try (then never looked back).

More and more people are now doing the same as me, including the **New Zealand 2015 Rugby World Cup Winning Team**. Famously, those amazingly tough New Zealand athletes attributed their great form to a diet that had a high proportion of coconut oil. Prior to adopting the LCHF diet, these professional rugby players were eating a low fat diet and some of their sporting results had been disappointing.

Around a quarter of the USA and UK adult population are now obese. 2 out every 3 adults in USA and UK are overweight. This situation is considerably worse now than it was 30 years ago when we all started adhering to low fat diets in the belief that we would be healthier as a result.

Influential policy-makers seem reluctant to adopt the growing evidence that eating fat is not the problem. Low-carbohydrate diets tend to be healthier and more effective for weight loss than low-fat diets. A recent article in the British Medical Journal (BMJ) provides great detail on this. http://www.bmj.com/content/351/bmj.h4962/rapid-responses

LCHF diet 'cured' a Brighton patient of type-2 diabetes in 8 weeks by following dietary advice of http://www.dietdoctor.com/lchf. I was impressed but not surprised when a patient's blood sugar levels dropped by over 20% (back into the normal range) without any medication. <u>Strictly speaking this is not a cure</u>, because the lifestyle change needs to be continued longterm. This strategy can greatly delay (sometimes by several years) the need to start diabetic medication or insulin injections.

Interestingly, this patient's cholesterol level dropped significantly despite adhering to this high fat diet. Also, there was a greater proportion of healthy HDL cholesterol, which is thought to actually protect the heart.

We should not be scared to eat fat because fat is a valid and important fuel for the human body. In the last 30 years, many of us have been replacing dietary fat with carbohydrate (either knowingly or without realising).

Low fat products usually have to include more carbohydrate (as a cheap filler ingredient and to compensate for the lack of flavour that tends to be a problem for low-fat foods).

Carbohydrate-rich foods such as bread, rice, potato and pasta have become abundant as a result of agricultural advances in the last few thousand years.

The modern human body is the same as the human body from hundreds of thousands of years ago.

Evolution is extremely slow and modern low-fat foods are not the diet that the human body is best suited to.

All carbohydrates are converted by our digestive system into glucose (blood sugar) within a short time and this glucose has to be rapidly stored away because high blood-sugar levels are harmful.

Our bodies produce insulin to keep the blood-sugar down. When the body cannot make sufficient insulin to manage the carbohydrate intake then the blood sugar level rises too high and this produces an illness called 'Diabetes'.

Constantly high levels of insulin (in response to high carbohydrate intake) induces growth of fat cells throughout the body. The fat cells are the energy stores where much of the carbohydrate/glucose is deposited once the body has turned it into fat.

Low carbohydrate diets with moderate or high fat content result in less insulin requirement. Lower insulin levels encourage the fat cells to release fat for use as fuel by the body.

Many long-distance athletes (such as marathon runners and triathletes) adhere to low carbohydrate diets to make themselves leaner and more efficient at using fat as fuel. These athletes may take glucose drinks during races for an extra boost but they are still getting a large proportion of their muscle energy during races provided by 'aerobic fat-burning'.

It takes about one week for our bodies to become better accustomed to using fat as the main fuel instead of carbohydrate. Once this adaptation occurs, we tend to not feel hungry between meals because we fuel on body-fat without noticing any change in energy level.

Importantly, better adaptation to using fat as fuel makes us less dependent upon the body's limited glycogen stores (plus race-day glucose in drinks and gels) during a marathon race. Therefore, we are less likely to 'hit the wall' towards the end of a marathon race.

"Which fats and oils are healthy?" is debated amongst experts and some disagreement remains. I aim to eat "real food" rather than food created by industrial processes (trans fats for example). Many people chose to eat mostly unsaturated fats (such as olive oil) as these have a better health reputation compared to saturated fats (such as butter) but personally I eat both these types.

LCHF diet can lower blood cholesterol levels, though this does not happen with everyone. The explanation is that our bodies make fat and cholesterol from carbohydrates and other foods. Indeed our bodies will routinely break down excess dietary protein to glucose, then make this into fat.

The fat circulating in the blood is known as 'blood lipids' or 'serum cholesterol'. High levels of lipids and cholesterol are often a sign that the body is not using fat as a fuel, so lipids and cholesterol are then like waste products that get harmfully deposited in places such as blood vessel walls (for example leading to blocked coronary arteries).

Therefore, it may be that if we adapt our bodies better to using fat as a fuel then we may actually clean our coronary arteries somewhat.

Athletes take nutrition very seriously. It was my great privilege to meet **Dave Scott** (6 times Ironman World Champion and highly successful coach) at the 2016 World Ironman Championship in Kona, Hawaii.

Dave was very generous with his time, talking to me about nutrition and other endurance sport topics. A truly great man. Dave coaches lots of athletes (World Champions themselves in some cases) and his web-site has lots of nutrition advice. http://davescottinc.com/high-performance-nutrition/

Protein in the diet

Protein intake should be kept at a moderate level for marathon runners. We need fat and oil to be the majority of our food intake because we need our bodies to be adapted to using fat as the main fuel.

If protein comprises the majority of our food intake, our bodies become adapted to using protein as the main fuel source. Then we will 'burn muscle' instead of 'burning fat' when dieting or during long exercise sessions (and marathons).

When we eat more protein than the amount needed as building material for body structures, then our bodies break down the excess protein to produce glucose. Our bodies do not simply store excess protein as bigger muscles.

Many endurance athletes adhere to a low carbohydrate, low fat diet that is very rich in protein. Unfortunately, they have misunderstood the principles of an ideal endurance athletic diet.

A high protein diet may or may not suit a bodybuilder or a sprinter, but such things are not currently my field of interest.

Ketogenic Diet

In the past this has primarily been used to treat epilepsy in children, especially when medication has not been effective. Any epilepsy management must be done under expert medical instruction, guidance and supervision.

Ketones can be used by the brain as a fuel instead of glucose and for some children the ketogenic diet prevents epileptic seizures.

The ketogenic diet is a high fat diet with low/ moderate protein and very low carbohydrate. The liver converts fat into fatty acids and ketones.

The ketogenic diet is the same as a rather extreme LCHF diet. Many coaches believe that the raised levels of ketones in the blood (ketosis) do seem to have an anti-inflammatory effect (which helps prevent or mend runner's injuries).

Some experts believe that the ketogenic diet has potential for helping treat or prevent cancer in some people. This theory is based upon the fact that many cancer cells have a high glucose demand. Restricting the access to glucose seems to hurt some cancer cells but healthy cells can tolerate this.

Further Reading

The Real Meal Revolution: The Radical, Sustainable Approach to Healthy Eating. By Professor Tim Noakes, Jonno Proudfoot and Sally-Ann Creed. Paperback May 17, 2016.
This bestseller, overturns the conventional dietary wisdom of recent decades that placed carbohydrates at the base of the supposedly healthy-eating pyramid and that has led directly to a worldwide epidemic of obesity and diabetes.

Is There Something In The LCHF / Ketogenic Diet For Endurance Athletes? By Martin Hill. Published October 6, 2016 in Triathlete Europe.
http://triathlete-europe.competitor.com/2016/10/06/something-lchf-ketogenic-diet-endurance-athletes

Ironman Legend Dave Scott Shares His Nutrition Tips. By Julia Polloreno. Posted On: Oct 24, 2016 at Triathlete.com
http://www.triathlete.com/2016/10/nutrition/ironman-legend-dave-scott-shares-nutrition-tips_295422

CHAPTER 6

Inspiration and
Inspirational People

2012 London Paralympics

It does seem that adapting to cope with the challenges of sport makes us more resilient to cope with other challenges in life.

Some people develop mental strength from having 'life deal them a difficult hand', and this toughness can make them excellent at sport.

This book is for runners of all ages and all abilities. Indeed, readers could progress from 'got a bad leg but just want to complete one marathon' to becoming 'elite'.

Eddie Izzard

New to running in 2009, Eddie completed 43 marathons in 51 days to raise money for charity. It was a remarkable achievement because this 47-year old celebrity had done very little training in preparation and was in pain most of the time.

Television audiences were amazed by his 1,100 miles of running. It was truly inspiring to see Eddie's cheerful courage and determination.

Many people, including me, were inspired by Eddie Izzard to go running. After seeing him keep running day after day despite his pain, I felt more able to persevere and ignore muscle aches.

Eddie ran 27 marathons in 27 days (across South Africa) in 2016 at age 54. Again he raised huge amounts of money for charity and he inspired many people. He looked fitter than in 2009 and he appeared to have become a good runner rather than the 'have a go hero' of 7 years earlier.

Eddie Izard is also famous for being a highly successful comedian, actor and writer. http://www.eddieizzard.com

Running and Triathlon Clubs

Maybe it is best not to mention individuals because they may get embarrassed. Also it may not be fair to mention some people and not others. Nevertheless, I have a small selection of examples for you to think about.

My club has an international age-group standard athlete (aged over 70) with joint replacements who goes training most days and always has a smile on his face.

Iron-distance Triathlon racing alongside a friend who has insulin dependent diabetes brings a whole new insight into the difficulties some people manage to overcome with race nutrition.

There are competitive athletes in the club who have come to triathlon following serious injuries from other previous activities.

Many contact sports result in injuries that end further participation in that sport, but that misfortune can herald the beginning of a wonderful triathlon career.

Triathlon makes predictable physical demands that we can deal with even if we have limiters or disabilities.

One very inspiring friend has constant pain from a paralysed arm and he has developed his own unique (highly effective) racing methods in order to overcome his problems. This makes me realise that I can overcome my own limitations and it is the "right attitude" that counts most.

One friend completed an iron-distance triathlon every day for 10 days, whilst in constant back pain from a prolapsed lumbar disc. The same friend ran 100 miles in an ultra-marathon running race, but did not get a medal because he got lost and did not run the correct 100 miles.

Very often the failures are more inspiring than the successes, perhaps because we then realise just how big the challenge was.

For instance, another of our club's ultra-marathon runners has repeatedly just failed to complete swimming the 22.5 mile English Channel (the tides and currents result in swimmers often spending more than 24 hours in the cold choppy water, swimming more than 50 miles).

There are presumably numerous running and triathlon clubs all around the world that are as supportive and inspiring as the club that I am proud to be a member of. Every runner should join their local club.

Co-Workers

Right at the beginning of my own adventures into marathon running, I drew inspiration from a co-worker (Chris) who, at age 50, ran the fastest marathon in the world for her age group for that year!

Chris had started running at age 30 (at the time that she quit smoking) and it took several sessions before she could complete a whole mile non-stop. After a year or so, she completed a 10k race, but it took her more than an hour.

A few years after starting running, a very creditable 3:56 Marathon was completed. Chris continued to improve and had a truly world-beating year in 2005 at age 50.

37:14 for 10k
1:23:01 for Half-Marathon
2:55:54 for Marathon

Chris is a warm-spirited working mother, who has been generous with her advice to help me improve at marathon running. She is under 5 foot tall, which shows that long legs are not an essential requirement for elite marathon running.

CHAPTER 7

Mind

Lava Tube, Big Island, Hawaii

'Dig deep' and tap in to your reserves of inner strength to find energy that you had not realised was there.

It is often said that **"the mind is the strongest muscle in the body"**.

The mind is not actually a muscle but (like muscles) it can be made stronger with training.

The decisive factor between athletes of similar ability is usually "mental strength".

Motivation

"Why am I doing this race or this training session?"
"How much do I want this?"

It is good to to have numerous small goals that will be milestones on your journey. It is powerful to have a big prize at the end that may take a few years to achieve. This combination of longterm, medium term and short term objectives will keep us motivated.

These are some of the common objectives:
1. Raise money for charity
2. Be a role model for other people (your kids perhaps)
3. Raise self-esteem
4. Improve health
5. Make the most of your god-given talent
6. Good-for-age qualification (Boston, London, Berlin, etc)

Resilience

The most successful people tend to be above average at dealing with set-backs. In fact, successful people are less afraid of failure.

Don't always stay in your comfort zone but do challenge yourself. Every failure is a learning opportunity.

Don't give up when you have an injury or a limiter. Find a remedy or an alternative method. Inspirational people are often great examples of these qualities.

The lessons in resilience gained from sport make us more able to cope with set-backs in everyday life.

Managing the Chimp

In his 2012 book "The Chimp Paradox", Prof Steve Peters describes a mind management model that is endorsed by elite athletes. Multiple Olympic Gold Medalist, Sir Chris Hoy, endorsed the book and says it helped him win Gold.

Our minds function as if we have a faster stronger irrational primate brain as well as a slower weaker logical human brain.

At times we can use our primate brain to help us do apparently superhuman things. At other times we must 'manage the chimp' and allow the human brain to rule us.

'Distracting the chimp' is an example of a technique that runners employ to allow their minds to produce a better running performance. At times our primate brain tells us to slow down or quit and the human brain is not strong enough to fight over the issue.

However, the powerful primate brain can be distracted by a small reward. Chimps like bananas. The reward we use to distract our primate thoughts could literally be a banana but an energy gel or a sip of water will do.

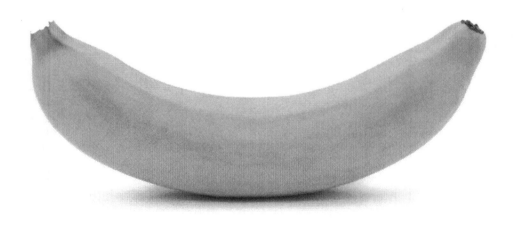

Tell the your 'inner chimp' to "keep running at this pace for another few hundred yards then you can have a reward". Other effective distractions include 'counting to twenty' or 'focusing on reaching the next mile-marker' or 'shadowing the runner in front'. A mantra can be used for this purpose and this is described later in this chapter.

There is a great deal more within Prof Steve Peters's book. It helps with a wide range of topics related to success, behaviour, happiness and life in general. It gives a good insight into how our minds function.

Mental Energy

As humans we have the ability to influence our own mental energy levels and also influence the energy levels of other people around us.

There will be times when it is best to be in the company of people who will boost our mental energy levels rather than drain them. There will be other times when we will benefit from the opposite effect and it is good to be brought back down to earth.

It is helpful to recognise how our habits and behaviours affect other people and how their behaviours affect us.

In the Peak Training phase and during Race Week, we need to maximise our reserves of mental energy in order to be in our best condition on Race Day.

Visualisation

We can make mental pictures with eyes open or closed. We can manipulate the associations in our minds between these mental images and other things such as emotions and sensations.

Runners can use visualisation to remedy issues from things such as anxiety, fatigue or pain. Keep mental files in your mind that are related to good performance, joy and success.

Visualisation can be very powerful and the more we do it the more effective it becomes. When you run a great race or have good day, make a mental file of this and practice visualising it.

Muscle Memory

Repetition of physical activities (such as running) consolidates pathways in the brain for memory and movement co-ordination. Neuromuscular (nerve and muscle) pathways in the rest of the body also become consolidated.

For runners these processes result in greater running efficiency and quicker reaction times to hazards such as running on uneven surfaces.

Good quality and sufficient quantity of sleep after exercise is important for maximising the muscle-memory improvements derived from training.

Improved muscle-memory reduces the conscious effort required for running and therefore delays the onset of fatigue from long distance running.

Better muscle-memory leads to faster movements and this allows increased running pace. This is vital for the the speed interval sessions.

Run like your life depends on it

Our brains are hard-wired to allow our bodies to do what will result in the optimum chance of survival in any given situation.

This is why our ancestors survived in a hostile world during many thousands of years leading up to today.

When an ancestor was chasing prey they would be 'hard-wired' to quit and save energy if the chase was proving too hard. This ancestor would have thought they could not keep running or go any faster and they had reached maximum effort.

However, if their life depended on it (if say a lion chased them), they would find another level of power/energy/determination to run like never before.

There is a considerable gap, between the effort level at which 'we think our lungs will burst' if we run any harder, and the actual effort level required to harm us.

Hard race finishes (and training that simulates these) are effective at letting us tap-in to that potential extra level of effort. That is one reason why it is advisable to incorporate regular races into your training schedule.

<u>Do please ask permission from your physician (doctor) before attempting to raise your heart rate this high.</u>

'Park run' organise free, weekly, 5km timed runs in a multitude of venues around the world. They are open to everyone. These runs are excellent for adding a competitive edge to your training and encouraging a short intense effort. https://www.parkrun.org.uk

Pearls of Wisdom

"It's not the size of the dog in the fight, it's the size of the fight in the dog". Mark Twain.

"Some sessions are stars and some sessions are stones, but in the end they are all rocks and we build upon them." Chrissie Wellington, A Life Without Limits: A World Champion's Journey.

"We can beat them, just for one day. We can be Heroes, just for one day". David Bowie, Heroes.

"It's been no bed of roses, no pleasure cruise. I consider it a challenge before the whole human race, and I ain't gonna lose". Freddie Mercury, We Are The Champions.

Mantra

A sacred word, sound or phrase is called a 'mantra' in Sanskrit, which is the primary spiritual and philosophical language in Hinduism.

Mantras are thought to have psychological and spiritual powers. For runners, mantras certainly can be powerful at harnessing mental strength and focusing the runner on getting their best possible athletic performance.

I use different mantras in different situations and at different stages of training or within a race.

These words and phrases have been accumulated over the last few years and each has a special meaning for me. Here they are:

1. **"Courage"**. Said in a French accent. This is what spectators say as encouragement at the Paris Marathon and the Marrakesh Marathon. It brings back some great personal memories and fortifies me.

2. **"Animo"**. This brings me wonderful memories of 'digging deep' and 'toughing it out' at as spectators shouted "Animo" at Ironman Barcelona and at Ironman Lanzarote.

Spaniards use the word at races to mean "Come on. Hold on. Snap out of it".

Animo literally means 'mind, soul, zest and courage' in Spanish and in Italian. The word also reminds me of 'Animal', which inspires me to tap in to the primate-power of my ancestors.

3. **"As the race gets longer, I get stronger"**. This is a well known phrase, but I do not know to whom this should be attributed. The Ironman Triathlons, an Ultra-Marathon and a Double Ironman Triathlon that I did in the past do give me confidence that the second half of any race ought to be 'my time to shine'.

4. **"When the going gets tough, the tough get going"**. This is a song that was co-written and originally recorded by Billy Ocean in 1985.

The phrase has been attributed to both Joseph P. Kennedy (JFK's father) and also Knute Rockne (American footballer).

5. **"You've got this"**. This is what spectators shout as encouragement in USA races.

It has particular resonance for me in the final quarter of a marathon, because in my mind I will not falter from this point onwards. The finish beckons and I can start to take risks in terms of raising the heart rate and burning energy reserves.

This phrase triggers my mental image of elation, as I completed the brutal 'natural energy lab' section of the Kona Ironman Run to then finish the last 6 miles with a big grin.

6. **"Good job"**. This is another terrific phrase that USA spectators shout as encouragement. It makes me feel happy to be alive and happy to be participating.

It is also recognition that the race is going well and I have tried my best.

7. **"Come on Jim"**. It is a real boost when spectators shout out a runner's name, so it is always best to display your name in big letters on your vest.

In the final mile or two, I am often in my own little mental world and I no longer hear the crowd. Sometimes the cheers of the crowd are so loud towards the finish that I cannot hear individual voices.

I will often repeatedly say "come-on-Jim, come-on-Jim, come-on-Jim" for long periods at this stage of the race in order to keep me pushing hard right up until the finish.

8. **"Freeeedommmmm!!"**. This is a famously rousing defiant outburst from 13th Century Scottish hero, William Wallace, in Mel Gibson's 1995 epic movie 'Braveheart'. It also reminds me of my dad, Lindsay William Wallace Graham.

9. **"Scream"**. Sometimes in the last 50 metres, I just scream. It's like a battle-cry. It is a final do-or-die effort to get a personal best (PB) time or finish in front of a rival runner. The scream unleashes an anaerobic fast-twitch muscle-fibre power surge. This will get you over the finish-line even when there appears to be no energy left.

CHAPTER 8

Body

Understand how your body works and what maintenance is needed to keep it functioning well. The views and methods in this section (and indeed the entire book) work for me, but you should get permission from your coach, therapist or physician before changing what you already do.

Ageing

Much of the fitness reduction that we attribute to ageing is actually due to de-conditioning caused by lifestyle issues. There are some physical changes due to ageing but these may not be as important to marathon running as most people think.

• Age in itself is not a limiter on performance for most runners. You can keep improving your marathon times as you age.

• To plan your marathon training and the mile-by-mile plan for the marathon race, you just need to know your maximum Heart Rate (HRmax) and your Target Marathon Finish Time.

• This book tells you how to know your own personal HRmax, and this number is influenced by but not directly dependent upon your age.

• If a reader's HRmax is significantly different than average for their age then they should follow the plans that are correct for their HRmax rather than age.

• The stated age range for this book is 18 to 75. However, I have the deepest respect for the men and women aged over 75 who run marathons or compete in iron-distance triathlons. I have raced alongside these amazing people and I am not intending to tell them how it should be done because they are special.

Warm-up

For optimum running efficiency our core body temperature needs to rise by around 0.5 celsius. Typically this takes 10-20 minutes of exercise and during this time our bodies are more prone to injury.

Before this warm-up is complete, we are less able to deliver oxygen to muscles so we employ the anaerobic system at a lower heart rate (HR) than when we are fully warmed-up. Failure to warm-up causes an increased chance of muscle/ligament damage as well as poor race performance from 'going anaerobic too early'.

Exercise

For best marathon performance you need to do a high volume of exercise but it really is not that excessive. Exercise is good for our health and our bodies have evolved to do a great deal more exercise than most people imagine.

The typical modern lifestyle is too sedentary to the extent that it often makes people ill. We should all get into a regular routine of increased activity. This includes walking and cycling as alternatives to using motorised transport.

Gradually our bodies can adapt to more and more exercise. Eventually, we could (if we had time and desire) do a 10-hour triathlon training day once a week and consider it routine. Then running marathons seems a lot easier. This high volume of exercise is not needed to complete a marathon and most people will do nowhere near this much.

Marathon training involves many hours of exercise but the bulk of this is at low intensity to build up endurance. Long training days become a normal day like 'a day at the office' or perhaps more like 'a day of manual labour'.

Exercise becomes an integral part of the lifestyle, so that some training is no longer called training. Turning commuting (to and from work) into exercise will greatly increase the possible volume of exercise done.

It certainly does not have to be all running, as there are also fitness gains possible with swimming, cycling and other activities.

Warm-down

It is worth spending the last 10 minutes of an exercise session at low intensity to help the lactate to be cleared from the muscles.

This can be a slow run or a spin on an exercise bike. A long spin session (perhaps 40 minutes) can be particularly helpful for muscle recovery if you can spare the time.

Stretching

Most runners have a regular stretching routine. This should be done when warmed-up or at the end of an exercise session. Stretching before warm-up could cause damage in some cases.

It is good for runners to stretch regularly for the following reasons:

1. Keep the muscles and tendons supple.

2. Prevent shortening of tendons as this reduces stride length and agility.

3. Encourage soft-tissues (muscles, ligaments and tendons) to adapt to being stretched. Muscles normally shorten (contract) when in use, but at times the opposite can happen when running. Downhill running is most likely to cause contracting muscles to lengthen.

4. Prevent or remedy muscle tightness or tension. Tight tense muscles are more likely to get injured.

Stretching only takes a few minutes and it is good to simply make a habit of it without necessarily thinking too much about it. Over time, the process becomes automatic.

There is probably no need to know the names of all the muscles and tendons, so these are not described in detail.

The five simple stretches that follow should deal with the important areas for most runners.

There are many other methods of stretching and managing musculoskeletal issues. Physical therapists can help with more expert guidance on these matters if need be.

1. Iliotibial Band (ITB) - This stretch helps treat or prevent a number of problems that cause pains in the back, hip or knee.

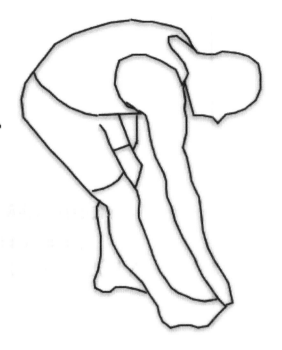

The ITB is a large region of tough fibrous tissue related to the muscles of the upper leg that connect the pelvis to the knee and shin. It is located on the outer side of the upper leg.

ITB tightness can adversely impact upon the movement and function of the knee to cause knee pains in some runners.

ITB inflammation can result in pains in one or more places in the back, hip or knee.

2. Stand on a step with the toes on the step and the heels off the back in order to stretch the Achilles Tendon and the Calf Muscle.

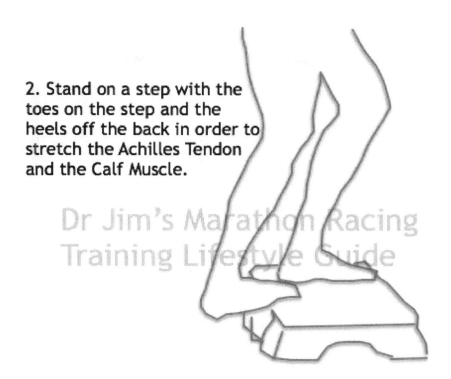

The **Achilles Tendon** is the thickest and strongest tendon in the body.

It needs to cope with large pulling forces from the calf muscles raising the heel against the entire bodyweight (pulling it in the opposite direction).

Good maintenance of the Achilles Tendon is a priority, because if it becomes injured or inflamed it <u>must</u> be rested.

This tendon is capable of completely tearing into two pieces, which is catastrophic for running (even in the long term potentially).

3. Lunge - This can be done in a static position that is held for a minute, whilst trying to lengthen the stride as much as possible. It can also be done as an active walking lunge if space

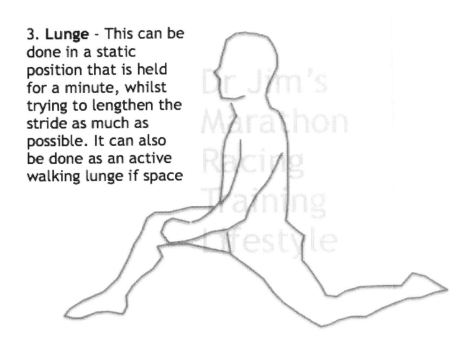

The Lunge helps to reduce tightness in several areas in order to allow the pelvis to project forwards for better running efficiency.

Stride lengthening from greater musculoskeletal flexibility is a component of faster paced running.

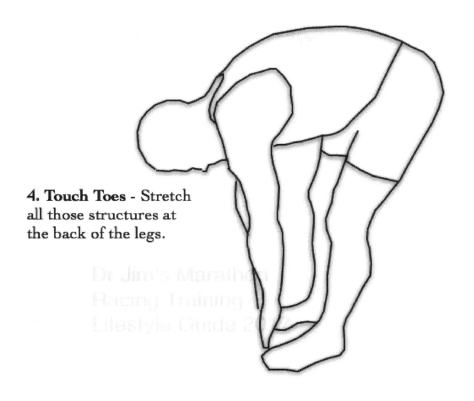

4. Touch Toes - Stretch all those structures at the back of the legs.

Touch Toes to prevent tightness in the hamstrings and lower back.

Removing tension from these areas is important for treating and preventing pulled hamstring and backache.

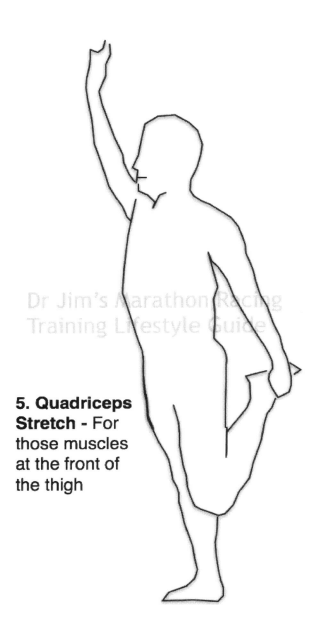

5. Quadriceps Stretch - For those muscles at the front of the thigh

Quadriceps Stretching can improve range of movement at the knee and at the pelvis, as well as relieving muscle tension at the front of the thigh.

Section B

"Get Set"

CHAPTER 9

Optimum Race Weight

The speed of marathon runners is strongly influenced by body weight. Most people will run faster marathons after they lose weight.

However, it is possible to lose too much weight. It is also possible to lose the wrong kind of weight.

Runners need robust bones, muscles, tendons, ligaments and numerous other things. Weight reduction requires the body to consume some of itself as fuel.

Ideally we want to consume body fat as fuel but preserve the other important components which are mostly made of protein.

The wrong kind of dieting will lead to more protein loss than fat loss. It is useful to monitor Body Fat Percentage in order to gauge that the right kind of weight loss is occurring.

Optimum race weight for each individual will vary. It is good to keep track of our weight and body fat data and see over time what works best for us individually (as judged by race results for instance).

Body Mass Index (BMI)

This is calculated as weight (kg) divided by the square of height (metres).

Underweight <18.5
Normal   18.5 - 25
Overweight   25 - 30
Obese   >30

Body Fat %

Men have a minimum healthy body fat of around 5%. This is known as essential body fat and it is required for all sorts of vital structures in the body including nerves. It is important not to have less body fat than this essential amount as running performance would suffer and illness would be likely to occur.

Women's bodies are rather different from those of men and the minimum (essential) body fat is much higher at around 10-13%. This fact is possibly the main reason that the women's world record marathon finish time is over 10 minutes slower than the men's world record.

male athletes have body fat at 5.5-13 %
female athletes have body fat at 13.5-19%

Scales

I use a Fitbit Aria Wi-Fi Smart Scale. It measures weight, body fat percentage and body mass index (BMI) to provide a full picture of weight trends. It is very easy to use.

I just stand on it for a few seconds whenever I undress to go in the shower. It automatically recognises me (compared to other people in our home who use the scales) and sends data to an app on my mobile phone.

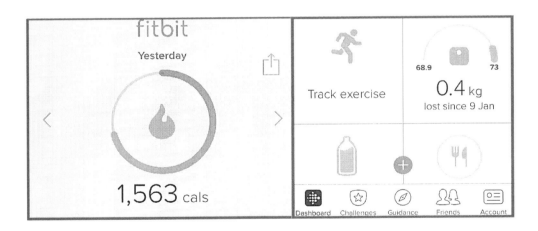

It is evident from the data that my body fat was optimal when I got my personal best (PB) marathon time in April 2016.

The BMI dipped in April (to just under 22). The lean body mass did not dip significantly and was at 62% when the body fat reached its minimum at 5%.

This indicates to me that the LCHF diet and marathon training was consuming body fat but preserving muscle. 5% body fat is unsustainable and undesirable for more than brief periods, so it soon returned to around 8%.

Weight during rest and recovery

The BMI and body fat scores rise during the December/January off-season when training is at a minimum and there is a lot of feasting. It would not be good to constantly remain at minimum levels of BMI and body fat.

Body Fat, Lean vs Fat, Weight and BMI

These 4 charts document the 12 month period from 1st January 2016 to 1st January 2017. Optimum weight and body fat occurred in the second quarter (April).

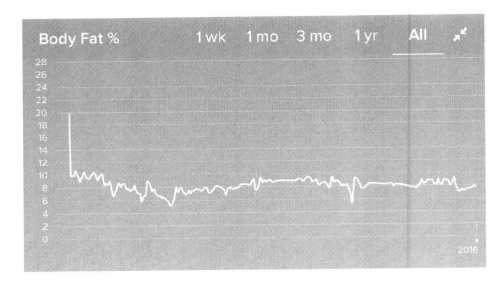

Jan Feb Mar Apr May Jun Jul Aug Sep Oct Nov Dec

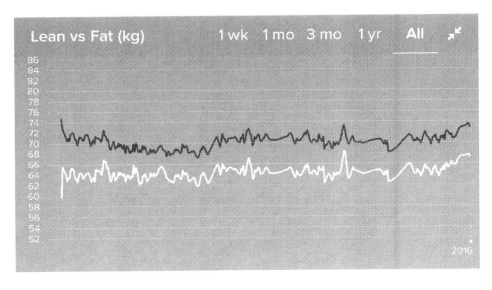

Jan Feb Mar Apr May Jun Jul Aug Sep Oct Nov Dec

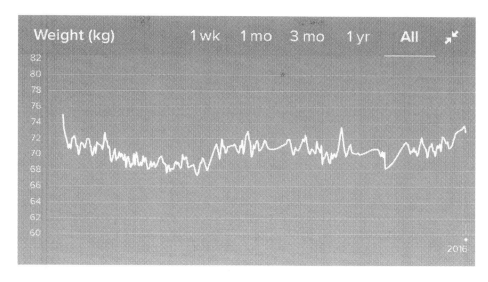

Jan Feb Mar Apr May Jun Jul Aug Sep Oct Nov Dec

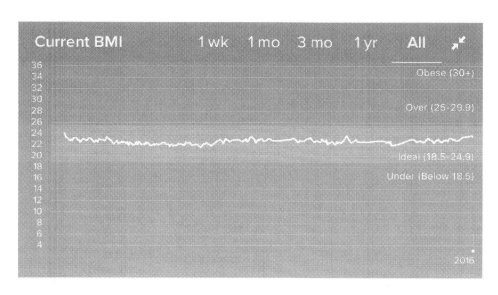

Jan Feb Mar Apr May Jun Jul Aug Sep Oct Nov Dec

CHAPTER 10

Injuries and Ailments

This is not a medical text book and perhaps 'runner injuries' will be the title of a future publication. This is clearly a huge topic. Listed in this chapter is a selection of the sort of problems that runners get.

Please bear in mind that these are mostly over-use injuries that have no permanent harmful effect on health.

Mostly these problems get better spontaneously over time, but they can be extremely annoying when they interrupt our training or impair our race performances.

Prevention is better than cure. Keep your toenails properly trimmed whilst running in the correct socks and shoes for your feet. Use lubrication.

Train with GRADUAL ADAPTATION and do not try to do too much too soon. Ease off training or do different training when injuries start to appear. Consult you coach, physical therapist or physician when a problem is apparent.

"A good runner leaves no tracks" according to Tao Te Ching by Lao Tzu 500BC (translated by Raymond B. Blakney 1955)

Common Running Injuries and Ailments

1. Runner's Knee

2. Blisters

3. Toenail Damage

4. Calcaneal Bursitis

5. Plantar Fasciitis

6. Achilles Tendinitis

7. Shin Splints

8. Back Ache and Muscle Strains

9. Iliotibial Band (ITB) Syndrome

10. Athletic Pubalgia (Gilmore's Groin)

11. Stress Fracture

12. "Stitch" (Side Cramp)

13. Sprained/Twisted/Turned Ankle

14. Patella Tendinitis

15. Chafing

16. Athlete's Foot (Tinea Pedis)

1. Runner's knee

Most runners will get knee pains from time to time and this is more likely with the high mileage training required for marathons.

There are several conditions (also known as disorders) with a variety of different names, that collectively are within the category of 'runner's knee'.

Patellofemoral Pain Syndrome, Anterior Knee Pain, Chondromalacia Patellae, Iliotibial Band Syndrome, and Plica Syndrome are the most commonly used terms to describe the different types of knee pain.

These knee pain disorders are related to repetitive movements and impacts on the knee joint caused by running.

Each runner is likely to have several contributing factors that are responsible for them getting knee pain.

Finding ways to reduce the effect of each of these factors will help each runner to minimise knee pains that they may get and prevent severe problems that will interrupt training.

Runner's knee is not strongly linked to subsequent development of arthritis and it is a shame that many people quit participating in running because of fears that severe damage is occurring when their knees ache.

The main **contributing factors** for Runner's knee are:

1. Increasing training demands on the body too rapidly.
2. Being overweight.
3. High impact running style.
4. Insufficient cushioning in the sole of the running shoe.
5. Poor mechanical function of the knee.

The main methods of **prevention and remedy** are:

1. Gradual adaptation rather than trying to do too much too soon.
2. Weight reduction.
3. Be light-on-your-feet. "A good runner leaves no tracks". Forefoot running makes the knee slightly bent at the moment when the ball of the foot hits the ground, resulting in shock-absorption by the Achilles Tendon and the muscles at the back of the leg. Forefoot running can be better for the knee than heel-strike running. When the heel strikes the ground first, the knee is usually locked in full extension and the impact of the foot hitting the ground is transmitted forcefully to the knee joint.

4. High running mileage on hard surfaces is best done with thick cushioned high quality running shoes. Alternatively do as much mileage as possible on soft ground.
5. There are numerous theories and ways of understanding knee pain that are related to imbalances or imperfect alignment of structures in the leg. A physical therapist should be able to help individual runners understand which of their muscles, ligaments or tendons need assistance. However, for the majority of runners, knee pain can be helped by strengthening the quadriceps muscle at the front of the thigh, and cycling is a highly effective method to do this. Most runners will benefit from a regular stretching regimen, as outlined in chapter 8 of this book.

2. Blisters

Blisters are collections of fluid under the top layer of skin caused by friction and rubbing.

Lubrication and correctly fitted high quality running shoes with good running socks should prevent blisters.

New shoes will usually require some breaking in, so use them for short periods intermittently over the first few weeks before wearing them for a long run.

3. Toenail Damage

Nail lifting or bleeding under the nail can be prevented by keeping toe nails trimmed and running in correctly fitting shoes.

Sometimes the shoe is too loose, causing the foot to repeatedly move forwards and impact the toes against the inner surface of the shoe. Tighter laces may be required.

There may not be enough space for the toes at the front of the shoe and a bigger size or a different shoe design with bigger 'toe-box' should be tried.

4. Calcaneal Bursitis

This condition causes pain at the back of the heel due to inflamed structures related to the join between the heel-bone and the Achilles Tendon.

The cause may be excessive forefoot running, resulting in more stress to these structures than they can cope with. Rest and avoiding forefoot running should assist recovery.

Anti-inflammatory tablets may help. Steroid injection into the Calcaneal Bursa can be used in severe cases but this is best done with ultrasound scan guidance, as steroid injection into the Achilles Tendon is best avoided.

5. Plantar Fasciitis

Plantar Fasciitis causes pain at the underside of the heel of the foot. This is not rare and it is more common in overweight people.

The underlying problem is scientifically complex but the prognosis is fairly good, as most cases get better within a year (with or without treatment).

Better footwear and reduced heel-striking may help. Anti-inflammatory tablets are often used and can be of benefit. In extreme cases a steroid injection under the heel may be needed to improve this condition.

6. Achilles Tendinitis (AT)

The Achilles Tendon connects the heel bone to the calf muscle. Any pain, swelling or tenderness of the Achilles Tendon must be taken very seriously.

This is the thickest and strongest tendon in the body but it has a relatively poor blood supply, so it is slow to mend.

Most concerning is the tendency for this tendon to completely rupture, thereby separating into two pieces. Achilles Tendinitis must be rested and it is not usually injected with steroid because that may increase the risk of rupture.

A health professional must be consulted when Achilles Tendon symptoms occur. Ruptured Achilles Tendon results in serious disability that usually requires surgical repair and many months of rehabilitation.

7. Shin Splints (medial tibial stress syndrome)

This is a common disorder that produces pain at the front of the lower leg related to the shin bone (tibia). The pain is worse with running and jumping, but there can be some pain when resting.

A stress fracture of the tibia can be mistaken for shin splints, but usually a fracture has a small area of intense pain and tenderness rather than shin splint pain which is spread over a region of several inches.

Shin splint pain is attributed to overuse injury of the fibres connected to the shin bone. Rest, ice and pain-relief tablets are used to stop the pain and promote recovery.

Gentle gradual return to running can occur when the problem has improved, but it is important to avoid doing too much too soon in order to avoid relapse.

Over-pronation (flat-feet or collapsed arch) is a recognised causal factor for shin splints. This can be remedied by running in shoes that support the foot arch and prevent over-pronation.

Forefoot running tends to stop over-pronation as well as reducing the impact forces on the shin bone.

Running on soft surfaces creates less impact on the shin bone compared to running on hard surfaces.

See a physician (doctor) if need be. Investigations such as MRI scan and bone scintigraphy may be required to exclude other conditions such as stress fracture, trapped nerve, trapped artery and compartment syndrome.

8. Back Ache and Muscle Strains

These common problems for runners will not be discussed in detail as they are predominantly self-evident conditions.

Prevention and management are by adherence to the good habits mentioned throughout this book.

The good habits include warm-up before running, stretching exercises, achieving ideal body weight, gradual adaptation, balanced training and good posture.

9. Iliotibial Band (ITB) syndrome

This condition results in pains in the knee, back, hip or thigh. Symptoms are related to tightness, damage or inflammation of fibrous tissue that connects groups of muscles on the outer surface of the hip and upper leg.

The ITB extends from the pelvis to below the knee. Rest, stretching and massage are often used to help remedy this problem.

10. Athletic Pubalgia (Gilmore's Groin)

Groin pain occurs during exercise, particularly with hip movements. There may be stiffness and soreness after exercise that can be worse the next morning.

Getting out of bed or getting out of a car seat may be painful. Groin pain may occur with coughing, sneezing or straining when lifting.

You should consult a physician (doctor) regarding these symptoms because diagnosis is difficult and investigations (such as MRI scan) may be required.

There are several possible underlying pathologies involved in this condition. Therefore, the best treatment for each individual case does require expert opinion.

Some cases may resolve with rest, physical therapy and stretching routines. Surgical repair is sometimes indicated but this is best avoided unless considered essential.

11. Stress Fractures

Stress fractures result from repetitive forces exerted on a bone rather than a single episode of large force. Any bone in the leg can develop a stress fracture but most commonly it is a foot long bone (metatarsal).

Typically, the bone develops tiny cracks at first rather than snapping into separate pieces. There is likely to be a specific place on the bone that is extremely painful when prodded.

When the fracture is recognised promptly and the bone is immobilised, it will usually mend within a few weeks.

Clearly, this is an injury that needs proper diagnosis and that will include an MRI scan or X-ray. This problem requires consultation with a physician (doctor).

The bone may need complete immobilisation in a cast in order to allow it to heal properly.

12. 'Stitch' or 'Side Cramp' (exercise related transient abdominal pain)

This condition is poorly understood, even by experts. The pain is most often on the right side of the upper abdomen, where the liver is located.

Theories about the cause are mostly related to blood flow issues and pressure changes caused by diaphragm movements with breathing in combination with the body jolting up and down with running.

Interestingly, swimmers can get 'stitch' symptoms even though swimming does not cause the body to jolt up and down in the same way that running does.

There are numerous suggested methods to deal with this problem. No method is 100% effective, but as the body adapts to regular running this disorder usually diminishes.

Prevention may be possible by avoiding eating for at least 2 hours before running, combined with a 20 minute warm-up routine. The liver, and structures related to it, are most active when digestion of food is happening.

Whilst running, avoid erratic breathing patterns and slow down running pace if 'stitch' symptoms appear.

13. Sprained/twisted/turned ankle

One or more ligaments of the ankle can be damaged if they are stretched excessively and this usually occurs suddenly rather than due to repetitive forces.

Ankle joint stability is weakened by damage to the ligaments that hold it together. Forefoot running can help as this reduces the tendency of the ankle to twist or turn. Over time the ligaments can strengthen with appropriate exercises.

14. Patellar Tendinitis (Jumper's Knee)

Pain in the tendon that connects the lower end of the knee cap to the upper part of the shin bone.

Stretching and thigh muscle strengthening exercises can be helpful. Anti-inflammatory tablets and steroid injections can be used.

A patellar tendon strap can provide relief for some runners.

15. Chafing

This is skin damage from friction and repetitive movement.

Prevention is by using lubrication and properly fitted good quality clothing.

16. Athlete's Foot (Tinea Pedis)

This is a fungus or yeast infection of the foot. The skin gets sore, itchy, reddened and splits.

It is treated with anti-fungal cream or anti-fungal capsules.

Severe cases of Athlete's Foot may become septic with secondary infection from bacteria, in which case antibiotic medication will be required.

Injury Prevention

Warm-up and Warm-down
Stretches after exercise
Balanced exercise regimen
Sleep and Rest days
Low volume of exercise at certain times in the year
Ketogenic diet (see nutrition section of this book)

Injury Treatment

You must consult your physician (doctor) for injury diagnosis, advice and management. However, if you chose not to do so there a few tips below:

The body mending itself

Some people have tremendous faith in the healing powers of doctors and therapists and some people believe none of this.

As a doctor, I understand that the body often mends itself but we need to make the situation optimal for that healing to happen properly and promptly.

A regular sustainable exercise regimen and healthy lifestyle goes a long way towards injury prevention and it helps injuries to mend.

Marathon training is mostly a matter of challenging the body (thereby doing some damage) with the expectation that the body will respond by rebuilding itself stronger and with adaptations that make it fitter to face the training challenge next time.

Medication

There is very little need for drugs and medicines for damage repair and adaptation to training challenges, so it is best to avoid these substances if at all possible.

This book has a section on illegal performance enhancing substances and needless to say these must never be taken or used. I do not believe that these substances would help anyway.

Sometimes the damage repair mechanisms of the body (known as inflammation) become excessive and harmful in their own right. In this situation, an anti-inflammatory medicine can be helpful. The ketogenic diet (that is discussed in the nutrition section) has an anti-inflammatory effect which may reduce the need for medication.

All medicines have potential side effects. Even the humble **non-steroidal anti-inflammatory tablet** called **Ibuprofen** can cause kidney damage and gastrointestinal bleeding.

Tragically a young marathon runner died at the Brighton Marathon in 2013. Media reports stated that the coroner implicated Ibuprofen as a principle cause of the fatal bleeding from his bowel. I work in Brighton as a doctor and this death caused great sadness, including in our running community.

Like many people I previously took Ibuprofen fairly often for things like sore legs, but now I rarely take it (certainly never around the time of a race).

Steroids

Steroids are potent anti-inflammatory medicines. In extreme cases, a steroid injection into (or near) a joint is justified for disorders such as calcaneal bursitis or plantar fasciitis.

This kind of steroid (glucocorticoid) is generally not a banned substance if permission has been granted for justifiable medical use https://www.wada-ama.org/en/questions-answers/therapeutic-use-exemption-tue.

Glucocorticoid Steroids do not promote muscle growth and in fact they tend to increase body fat and cause muscles to shrink.

Very different are the 'anabolic steroids' that promote muscle growth and these are all banned substances. Bulked up muscles are of no benefit to marathon runners anyway.

Creams, Lotions and Ointments

It is good to have a supply of topical (applied to the skin) treatments for prompt management of minor skin disorders. Early treatment of minor problems can prevent them becoming severe and an interruption to training.

Anti-fungal cream (such as clotrimazole) is most often used for inflamed skin creases and flexures. These areas favour the growth of yeasts and fungi. Runners are prone to this problem anywhere on the foot, but particularly between the toes. It can also be an issue in anogenital areas and the underpants region generally.

Antibiotic cream (such as Fucidic acid) can be used for cuts, grazes, blisters and chafing if they start to become septic. More severe bacterial infections will require antibiotic tablets or injections, so prompt use of an antibiotic cream can be of great value.

Lubricants (such as petroleum jelly) become of greater importance with longer runs and higher mileage training schedules.

Many runners have a regular routine of lubricant application before each run. Some runners carry a supply of lubricant with them for use during marathon races and at some events there is a supply of lubrication available at certain places on the course.

Feet and nipples usually need lubrication, but any area where a runner tends to experience chafing should be lubricated.

Physical Therapies

Physiotherapy, osteopathy, chiropractic, massage and other physical therapies can all be helpful with injury prevention and recovery.

Advice about posture, stretches and exercises can be extremely effective.

The power of manipulation may be overstated by some people, because ultimately the body tissues themselves have to do the actual healing.

CHAPTER 11

Goals and Year Planning

New York Marathon 2015

It is good to 'enjoy the moment' and not be constantly thinking about where you would rather be. This should be balanced against the benefits of planning and having goals.

Many people will go for regular runs or other forms of exercise and have little interest in competitions or personal best (PB) finish times. That's fine because these activities can provide huge benefits to health, happiness, friendships and overall wellbeing.

However, it does add another dimension to all this activity when we set goals and have strategies to hit these targets.

IRONMAN GOLD ALL WORLD ATHLETES PLEASE JOIN US FOR BREAKFAST IN KONA!

DATE: TUESDAY OCTOBER 4, 2016
TIME: 7:30-10 AM
LOCATION: SPLASHERS GRILL
75-5663 PALANI RD. KAILUA-KONA

CHOICE OF JUICE, COFFEE, TEA, OR SODA. FRESH FRUIT, YOGURT AND GRANOLA. SCRAMBLED EGGS, BACON, SAUSAGE, COUNTRY POTATOES AND BANANA MAC-NUT FRENCH TOAST.

MEET AND GREET SPECIAL GUESTS DAVE SCOTT, MARK ALLEN AND HALL OF FAME INDUCTEE PETER REID

RSVP HERE

This book will help you maximise your athletic potential and train most efficiently to achieve amazing results. Everyone has their own personal back-story and current circumstances.

We can all have healthy competition within our friendship groups, sports clubs and global peer group. We are all making exciting journeys of discovery and achievement that are specific to us personally.

This book and the methods described are applicable to those who are at the beginning of their athletic journey, and also applicable to those who are well advanced. Like me, some of you may have become runners in middle age and every race is still a PB opportunity.

Some of you may have been sports-stars in your youth and ageing makes you think that you cannot better your achievements of the past; but maybe you are wrong about that?.

There are many levels of current ability and there will always be other people who are better than us. It is terrifically rewarding to make progress upwards through these levels of ability and it is fine that we will never actually reach the top and become world champions.

However, in sports like marathon running and long distance triathlon we can actually race alongside world champions.

Goal-setting, planning and succeeding in sport makes us more prepared to succeed in life generally.

Overcoming set-backs and failures in sport makes us more resilient so that we cope better with problems and disappointments in life generally.

Case Study - Dr Jim's Goal History

Back-story
Represented school at cross-country running, but not best amongst school friends and not county standard.

Not a swimmer and not a cyclist.

Did not participate in sport after leaving school.

Fractures and ligament damage to foot and ankle in a motorcycle accident.

Ligament and cartilage damage to knee in a skiing accident.

Took up mountain-biking to tone-up thigh muscles as therapy for the bad knee.

Prior to 2008, the focus was on family and career. There had been very little desire to participate in sport or consider adhering to a healthy lifestyle. Like many people, attitudes changed from age 40 onwards.

Pre-2008
Goal - Complete a 100mile off-road cycle in 1 day (the South Downs Way) - **Done**

2008

Goal - Complete a Sprint Distance Triathlon (swim 400m, cycle 25km, run 5km) - **Done**

Goal - Complete a Half Marathon (13.1 miles) - Done

Goal - Complete a Marathon (26.2 miles) - **Done**

2009

Goal - Complete an Ironman Triathlon (swim 3.8km, cycle 112miles, Run 26.2miles) - **Done**

Goal - Qualify for London Marathon with good for age time - **Not Done**

Goal - Run 10k sub-40 mins - **Done**

2010

Goal - Complete an Ironman Triathlon sub-12 hours - **Not Done**

Goal - Qualify for London Marathon with good for age time - **Not Done**

Goal - Run Half Marathon sub-1:30 mins - **Not Done**

2011

Goal - Complete a Double Ironman Triathlon (swim 7.6km, cycle 224miles, Run 52.4miles) - **Done**

Goal - Qualify for London Marathon with good for age time - **Done**

Goal - Run Half Marathon sub-1:30 mins - **Done**

2012

Goal - Complete an Ironman Triathlon sub-11 hours - **Done**

Goal - Run Marathon sub-3 hours - **Not Done**

Goal - Run Half Marathon sub-1:20 mins - **Not Done**

2013

Goal - Qualify for Ironman Triathlon World Championship in Kona - **Not Done**

Goal - RunMarathon sub-3 hours - **Done**

Goal - Run Half Marathon sub-1:20 mins - **Not Done**

2014

Goal - Qualify for Ironman Triathlon World Championship in Kona - **Not Done**

Goal - Run Marathon sub-2:50 hours - **Not Done**

Goal - Run 10k sub-38 mins - **Done**

2015

Goal - Complete an Ironman Triathlon sub-10 hours - **Done**

Goal - Qualify for Ironman Triathlon World Championship in Kona - **Not Done**

Goal - Run Marathon sub-2:50 hours - **Not Done**

2016

Goal - Qualify for (and complete) Ironman Triathlon World Championship in Kona - **Done**

Goal - Run Marathon sub-2:50 hours - **Not Done**

Goal - Run 3 Marathons within a month (each sub-3 hours) - **Done**

2017 (this book published January 2017)

Goal - Run Half Marathon sub-1:20 mins

Goal - Run a Marathon sub-2:50 hours

Goal - Run 4 Marathon Majors (Boston, London, Berlin, Chicago) in same year (each sub-3 hours)

Goal - Represent Home Nation (Age Group Team) at Triathlon Long Distance ITU World Champion

Comments about these goals

1. Realistic, but challenging.

2. Appropriate for level of fitness and experience.

3. Some were achieved in-year, but some took years to achieve.

4. Some are right at the limit of potential and may never be achieved (e.g. sub-1:20 Half Marathon). Currently plateaued at 1:22.

5. Initially it is a goal simply to complete a race but later completing this distance is routine so the finish time becomes the new goal.

6. Triathlon is a very inclusive sport and most people can aspire to represent their Home Nation eventually (Regional Championship or World Championship).

7. A variety of different goals each year provides a fresh focus for each year.

Don't put 'all your eggs in one basket'

Each year have several main races that are goal achievement opportunities. There will be good days and bad days at racing.

There will be good months and bad months during training. A much anticipated race can be spoiled by catching a virus or straining a muscle.

In certain events we might already be near to our potential best, so it may require a massive training effort to achieve a tiny improvement. Therefore, we should also be developing new goals alongside our existing ones.

Focus vs. Variety

Successful people tend to focus their efforts in one direction and persist with these efforts for a long time. Successful people tend to keep trying and training, despite set-backs or failures.

Variety is good because it makes life more interesting and challenges us in different ways that create a richer stimulus for our bodies and minds to improve. However, too much variety could be a distraction from the focus on our main goals.

Grade A Races (our high priorities for the season)

It is good to enter races that occur during any month of the year. However, we will be at a peak of marathon fitness for just a few weeks each year. Typically this will be for a few weeks in late Spring and again for a few weeks in the Fall (Autumn).

It is best to have at least two Grade A races during each of these periods. For instance, one might enter a couple of flat fast marathons in April then another couple of similar races in September/October.

It is a myth that one cannot race another fast marathon, having already run a fast marathon within the previous few weeks.

Unexpected set-backs can occur at any time, so it is best to have at least two opportunities to get a fast time during each period when we are at peak marathon fitness.

The weather may be poor or we may just 'have a bad day' for one of the Grade A races, so it is good to have another Grade A race soon afterwards in order to make the most of all the training that was done in the previous months.

Grade B Races (our low priorities for the season)

It is advisable to have regular races throughout the year for numerous reasons. Racing every few weeks helps to dial-in pre-race preparations and minimise harmful effects of pre-race nervousness. Also:

1. Fun - no stress involved and just enjoy the event

2. Socialising - a group from your club is doing this event so it is a great opportunity to spend time with existing friends and maybe make new friends

3. Practice for a grade A race - dial in all the little things that need perfecting by having 'a dress rehearsal'

4. Top-up maximum effort adaptations - you seldom try as hard in training as you do in a race

5. Test new kit or new techniques - take the opportunity to find out if the stuff works in a race

6. Pace a friend to help them get a PB or age-group qualifying time - be prepared to hear bad language as they react against your constant "encouragement"

7. Support your local race organisers - these events are the life-blood of the sport

8. Doing something different - there are many variations of endurance sport and running so we don't want to miss out on these experiences

Volunteering and Marshalling

It is a genuine privilege being able to race. We should not take this for granted. It is good to volunteer to help out with races whenever possible.

Be a giver as well as a taker. All the races we enter require volunteers.

So much joy and inspiration comes from cheering-on other people. This helps us maintain the enthusiasm that is needed to keep doing all the training that marathons demand.

Volunteering and Marshalling at a local race

CHAPTER 12

Lifestyle

There are numerous systems of the human body and the human mind that can be adapted and improved in order to obtain better athletic performance.

Different types of training have different effects on these different systems. A good training strategy will have a positive effect on all of these systems.

This is more than simply a training schedule. It is a whole lifestyle. This lifestyle is wonderful and it helps generally with health, happiness and overall wellbeing. It is a great way to make new friends and get positive energy from inspirational people.

Marathon training plans typically advise 12 to 16 weeks of marathon preparation. The more successful runners incorporate this within an athletic lifestyle that spans many years.

There will be phases of relative rest or low intensity low volume unstructured activities, but training never really stops. The hard-won adaptations and fitness gains must not be allowed to leak away.

Maintaining a fitness regimen in the longterm can actually help our bodies resist injury. Many athletes find they are more prone to injury when coming back from excessively long periods away from training.

It is good to plan the main races each year around family holidays and the seasons within our environment. A typical year could comprise:

December - General Rest and Family Time

January - Base Training for Marathon and Triathlon

February - Build Training for Marathon

March - Peak Training for Marathon

April - Taper and Marathon Racing

May - Rest from Running but Build Training for Triathlon

June - Peak Training for Triathlon

July - Taper and Triathlon Racing

August - Rest and Family Holiday (including swimming, cycling and running)

September - Marathon Racing and/or Triathlon Racing

October - Marathon Racing and/or Triathlon Racing

November - Marathon Racing and/or Triathlon Racing

December - General Rest and Family Time

Managing to find time to do training

We do find time for the things that we really want to do. Once marathon training becomes the priority, it is generally possible to fit it all in.

It is essential to get the goodwill and support of our family, friends and colleagues.

So long as we fulfil our important commitments then those around us will accept that we will have to 'say no' to certain other things that may clash with the training schedule. We then have licence to decline extra duties or not 'stay for another drink'.

Some training can be squeezed in amongst other activities in a very time efficient way. For instance, we can get up 45 minutes earlier and do a 45 minute run from our doorstep (or on our home treadmill) as soon as we get out bed, then shower and dress for work as usual.

If we want to do 10 miles of running but we don't have a 2 hour free period in our day, we can split this into two runs. 5 mile run before breakfast then 5 mile run when we get home from work in the evening.

A regular routine for training is helpful for several reasons. After about 3 weeks, any regular routine becomes almost automatic so we tend to just get on and do it without much mental effort.

Our established routine is important for days when we have to drag ourselves out of bed whilst we are tired and the weather outside is unpleasant.

Also, the routine soon gets known by people around us, so they know not to expect us to be available during certain time-slots e.g. Sunday afternoons (long run day) or any weekday evening except Monday (rest day).

This 'protected time' for training is important to us. We earn the right to have this by generating "good will" as a result of being unselfish in other aspects of our lives.

Put your heart and <u>sole </u>into it

When running becomes one of your priorities, you are likely to find the time to do what is required to improve.

With a systematic logical approach, it is even possible to spend less time training and still get better results. This can happen when the quality of training is good and there is a healthy lifestyle to consolidate it.

CHAPTER 13

Sleep and Recovery

Rest

Resting is a vital part of training. This is the phase when the body responds to the challenges (and damage) posed by training, in order to re-model itself.

This re-modelling makes the body, stronger and better adapted to cope with future challenges.

When recovery is of poor quality or of insufficient quantity, the benefits of training are not fully achieved plus injury is more likely.

Effects of Sleep

Sufficient good quality sleep is important for a wide range of reasons. Sport and exercise is good for promoting healthy sleep patterns. To be good at sports it is necessary to sleep well.

From an athletic performance viewpoint, sleep is vital for developing 'muscle memory' (neuromuscular pathways) required for good technique and form.

During sleep, our bodies do the majority of the physical repairs and rebuilding that are needed for fitness gains. More sleep means more 'fitness and form'.

Over-training

If the correct balance between training and recovery is not achieved, our bodies can become 'over trained' and performance deteriorates.

Over-training needs to be recognised promptly so that increased rest and recovery strategies can be implemented to remedy the situation.

Device-detox

Keep your mobile phone and other communication devices away from the bedroom.

Make your bedroom into a 'rest-cocoon'. Improve sleep quality by resting the brain and removing distractions.

Set aside specific times in the day when you deal with emails and social media. Avoid emails and messaging in the hour before bed-time, but it is alright to a read a book or an eBook.

Place a notebook and a pen at your bedside, so that if anything is occupying your mind you can make a note of it then forget about it until you awaken the next morning.

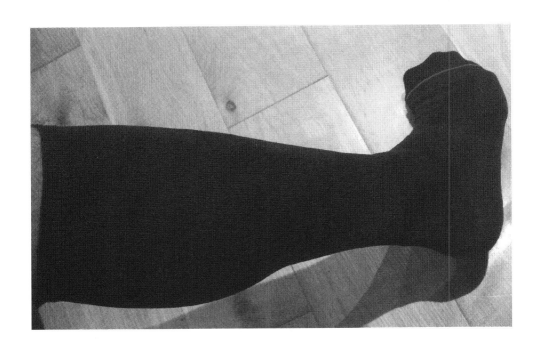

Compression clothing

In theory compression clothing improves blood flow through muscles by compressing the veins in the skin, thereby diverting blood flow to deeper veins.

This is something that I do believe in, particularly for the calf-muscles and thigh muscles.

I wear compression shorts and long compression socks. I wear this compression clothing for training, racing and recovery.

More blood flow to and from the muscles may improve lactate clearance whilst racing as well as after the race, in my view.

CHAPTER 14

Biggest Bang for Your Training Buck

Build a more powerful engine but also lose weight

Athletic training is a bit like transforming an average family car into a racing car. What modifications would be worth doing to make the car go faster? The car solutions are obvious.

1. Remove all excess weight
2. More powerful engine
3. Tune the engine
4. Upgrade suspension, steering and brakes
5. Good maintenance

Similar processes are used to make speed improvements to the marathon runner's body.

Weight reduction

This potentially costs nothing extra beyond your regular outgoings and indeed food spend could be reduced. See the nutrition and recipes sections.

If you did nothing else so that your 'engine' got no more powerful, you would run faster simply by being lighter.

Weight loss consumes none of your precious time and the weight can trickle down as you continue with your normal day to day activities. See the nutrition and recipes sections (chapters 5 and 17).

If you are limited by injury or cannot increase your volume of training for any reason, then focus on weight reduction and you could be amazed by the results.

See the section on optimum race weight (chapter 9). Successful athletes tend to have a significantly lower body fat percentage compared to the average population and this is not a coincidence.

Balanced training schedule

Build your body a more powerful 'engine' from the base upwards. This literally starts with base-training then proceeds to build-training as outlined in chapter 18.

The 'engine' is the physical power-plant of the body. This is principally the heart, lungs and leg muscles.

Within human cells are tiny 'mitochondria', that are fundamental to the release of energy. Faster running pace requires greater release of energy within the muscle fibres of the legs and the heart.

The quantity and quality of the mitochondria is improved with training. These improvements raise the runner's power production without necessarily making the muscles bigger in size.

The body's power output can be measured by various means but a commonly used method is called VO2max.

There is no need to actually measure the power output of the body and most athletes do not bother because they can monitor athletic ability improvements by other simpler methods (described later).

High training volume

This has the effect of upgrading most of our 'car's components'.

It is very worthwhile to run at least 40 miles weekly during Peak Training. Increasing this Peak Training mileage to 60 brings further benefit.

Small improvements will occur for every increase in weekly Peak Training mileage between 60 and 100, but this may not be possible due to repetitive stress running injuries.

It may be better to add more cycling and swimming to increase training volume rather than cause running injury from too many miles run.

Grade B Races

These are like 'dress rehearsals' and they 'tune the engine' with higher efforts than we can achieve with routine training sessions.

Nutrition

As described in the nutrition section of this book, there is considerable benefit from correct everyday nutrition.

On race day, we need to have optimum ability to use body-fat as a fuel (using the aerobic system) because there is a limit to how much we can use the anaerobic system.

Adaptations created by everyday nutrition and training can make our metabolism optimised for marathon racing.

Kit

Lighter shoes require a tiny bit less effort to run with, compared to standard shoes. This effect is significant in running races.

There are small benefits to be had from better quality kit generally but race day is not the occasion to try these things for the first time.

It is best to do the training running miles in the heavier highly cushioned shoes that reduce the risk of injury. The light-weight racing shoes are best used for special occasions.

Sleep

During sleep the body makes positive adaptations in response to training and repairs damage. This is an essential part of the training regimen and is rather like 'essential car maintenance'.

Aim for at least 8 hours of good quality sleep each night and maybe more than this following high volume training or marathon racing.

Good quality sleep is not provided by sedatives such as alcohol or sleeping tablets. 4 hours of 'clean sleep' is better than 8 hours of sedative-induced sleep. This is particularly true for neuromuscular pathway (muscle memory) fitness gains.

Methods to monitor athletic ability changes
VO2max

VO2max is the highest rate of oxygen consumption possible for an individual at a particular time in their training. It does not remain constant and it reflects the current aerobic fitness level.

VO2max requires special equipment to measure precisely, so for most people this is not a practical

good
neuro-
muscular
pathways

high
VO2max

powerful
mitochondria

method to gauge day to day aerobic fitness. However, estimates of VO2max are possible by (running or cycling) time trials combined with some mathematics. Some of the more expensive GPS watches do now feature VO2max estimates as a built-in feature.

Many people think it is more practical to simply monitor their time trial performances to monitor their fitness levels, rather than use VO2max.

Time trials

A time trial is a shorter than race distance run that can be done regularly on the same course (or route) in order to monitor fitness level and response to training.

This should ideally be a set measured distance on a good surface that is relatively flat and free of obstacles. The time trial should be run with 100% effort. It could, for instance, be a 200m to 1 mile section that you come across on your regular training run.

I have a 1 mile section that I like to run flat-out and it is located at the penultimate mile on my way home. This gives me an indication of current fitness status and I like to try to do it under 6:25 (when I am at peak fitness). It also simulates the penultimate mile of the marathon (if I do it towards the end of the weekly long run).

Power meters

I have used a power meter for cycling training in recent years and found it very helpful to monitor effort levels during workouts as well as fitness gains throughout the training schedule.

Recently, <u>running power meters</u> have arrived on the market and these will presumably offer the same benefits to runners that cyclists have been experiencing for years. Presumably a running power meter will be a useful tool for making VO2max estimates.

I have not yet used a running power meter myself. I would like to try one for training but perhaps I would avoid using one for racing because of the small, but maybe significant, weight increase from the device.

There is an article regarding running power meters at this web address: <u>http://www.runnersworld.com/ask-coach-jenny/a-guide-to-running-power-meters</u>

Power = Work ÷ Time
Power is the rate of doing Work.
Power is the amount of energy consumed per unit of time.
Power is expressed in **Watts**, which are equivalent to **Joules per Second**

CHAPTER 15

Marathon Training Plans

Variety

It is best to stimulate all the relevant body systems in order to obtain the adaptations that improve athletic ability.

There are other ways of describing these body systems but the list below is fairly comprehensive:

Speed

Endurance

Lactate Threshold

Form

Cardiovascular status

Mental status

Metabolic status

Musculoskeletal status (including core strength)

Balance

Getting the optimal balance between training on these different body systems will depend upon the current abilities and weaknesses of each individual as well as their current goals.

For example, to improve running it can be helpful to do some swimming. However, too much swimming might not be desirable. Swimming improves cardiovascular fitness and endurance without stressing the muscles, ligaments, bones and tendons that are prone to overuse injuries in runners.

We have a finite amount of available time for training so we must not neglect our key running training sessions.

Core body strength gained from swimming helps runners to have better posture and form, but massive upper body muscles from lots of swimming might be excess weight for a runner.

Forty 'push ups' (otherwise known as 'press ups') each day will only take a couple of minutes, but they will promote good core body strength. Make this part of your daily routine to help good running form.

12 to 16 week Marathon Training Plans

To complete a marathon we need a lot of endurance and this is what the majority (maybe 80%) of marathon training must address.

To run faster marathons we need to maintain the endurance adaptations whilst improving all the other body systems.

Principally, there are 4 phases that last up to a month each. Base, Build, Peak and Taper.

Then there is the Recovery phase (that starts the moment we cross the Race Finish Line).

If time is short and you are already adapted to running marathons, then you could omit/reduce the Base Training. It could then become a 12 week training plan.

If time is short and you are not already adapted to running marathons, then I suggest that you omit weeks 1, 5, 8 and 11.

Base Training - 100% aerobic
Weeks 1-4

Build Training - 90% aerobic and 10% anaerobic
Weeks 5-9

Peak Training - 70% aerobic and 30% anaerobic
Weeks 10-13

Taper and Race - 80% aerobic and 20% anaerobic
Weeks 14-16

Recovery - 100% aerobic
Post-Race

Training Running Mileage

There are exceptions but generally, faster marathon finish times come with increased training running mileage.

It is important to build up gradually to high weekly training miles to allow the body enough time to adapt and avoid injury.

The high training mileage mentioned below need only be for 3 to 4 weeks during the Peak Training phase.

The 'law of diminishing returns' applies to training mileage. There is a huge benefit from running 40 miles each week compared to running just 20. There is a reasonable improvement in marathon finish time as a result of increasing weekly training mileage from 40 to 60.

Modest improvement will be derived from increasing weekly mileage from 60 to 80, but this modest gain could be exactly what you need in order to get your goal finish time.

Weekly training mileage above 80 may not be possible for everybody, and indeed it may not be beneficial for everybody due to over-training risks.

However, it might be fun to achieve at least one training week of 100 miles, just to be able to say you 'once did it'. My maximum so far has been 80 miles and this was followed shortly afterwards by my 2:51 PB (personal best).

It is inadvisable to attempt very high weekly running mileage if you are currently carrying too much weight, as injury risk will be too high. It would be better to run 40-60 miles each week plus focus on dieting, swimming and cycling.

Running on soft-ground or on treadmills will generally be less damaging, so it helps to do a lot of the training with these methods rather than always running on roads or paving.

Balanced Training

High training running mileage alone will not be sufficient to achieve a fast marathon race finish time. Most of these miles should be at easy effort with HR in Zone 1-2.

However, there will need to also be sprint interval training and some race-pace efforts. Specific details are in the training schedules that are to be found later in this chapter.

The marathon training schedules in this book have 3 main types of run that need to be done each week (Long Run, Intervals Run and Tempo Run). It is best to separate these key workouts with rest days or days of less important (less demanding) training.

The long run is crucial each week and the schedules assume this day will be each Sunday, but the days of the week could be adjusted if your personal timetable means that you need to do your long run on a different day.

It is good to incorporate a Half-Marathon (HalfM) race around 7 weeks prior to the Marathon race that is the end-point of the 16 week training schedule. This should be done at 100% effort and it is a personal best (PB) opportunity.

This HalfM Finish Time is very useful for calculating Marathon Race Day Pacing. See the section of this book regarding calculating Target Marathon Pace and Target Marathon Finish Time.

Running Twice in a Day

Some people find it suits them to split the day's running requirement into a morning run plus an evening run. This can fit in with domestic commitments and work commitments.

This is often necessary if you are running more than 60 miles in a week. However, it is best to do the longest run of the week as a single continuous run because this is important for endurance adaptations to occur.

There can be less stiffness for the second run of the day compared to a run the next day. This is because the body's inflammatory response to exercise can take 12 hours to fully establish. Therefore, it is sometimes better to do 2 days worth of running training in a single day then recover without running on the following day.

Tempo Run

10 minute warm-up run followed by a moderately fast even effort run at around your lactate threshold (LT).

The LT is the threshold above which the waste-products of the anaerobic system will rapidly build-up and accelerate fatigue.

Tempo runs encourage adaptations that raise the LT and allow faster running for longer without excessive fatigue.

During the tempo run you are too breathless to talk with ease but it is not uncomfortable to run at this pace for an hour.

Your Heart Rate (HR) will be around 25bpm lower than maximum (HRmax-25). This is the borderline between Z3 and Z4. This is a similar pace to your potential best marathon average pace.

Do the penultimate mile at target marathon race pace. 10 minute warm-down to finish followed by stretching and preferably 10 minutes spinning on an exercise bike.

Intervals Run

10-20 minute warm-up run followed by between 3 and 7 sprint intervals. It can be particularly effective to do these runs on a treadmill.

These brief periods of upper Z4 maximum effort sprints (lasting 1 to 2 minutes) are separated by recovery periods of Z1 running (lasting 2 to 3 minutes).
<u>Do please ask permission from your physician (doctor) before attempting to raise your heart rate this high.</u>

These runs improve running efficiency and form by improving neuromuscular pathways (muscle memory). Also the mind and body become more tolerant of hard effort so that more fatigue can be endured in a race.

10 minute warm-down to finish followed by stretching (and preferably 10 minutes spinning on an exercise bike).

RnR (Rest and Recovery)

This can be complete rest if you are feeling exhausted and this is often the case on the day after the longest run of the week.
Alternatively, RnR could be spinning on an exercise bike or swimming.

Z1-2 Run

Exclusively aerobic exercise in Zones 1 to 2. Important to not let HR rise above HRmax-65.

Z2 Run

Predominantly aerobic exercise in Zone 2 with HR kept below HRmax-50.

Z3-4 Run

Generally, Zone 3 is avoided during marathon training because it employs the anaerobic system too much for our needs.

The Z3-4 run occurs when we race a half-marathon but this only happens once during the 16 week schedule. There is a 10 minute pre-race warm-up, then the race is run throughout with HRmax-25 and finishes with a sprint finish at HRmax.

Do please ask permission from your physician (doctor) before attempting to raise your heart rate this high.

Z2-4 Run

This is for the long runs during Peak Training and During Taper. Most of the running is in Zone 2 at around HRmax-60to50, but the penultimate mile is run a Zone 4 sprint at HRmax-10. The final mile is in Zone 2 at around HRmax-60.

* Both Zone 2-3 and Zone 3 tend to be avoided for marathon training and marathon racing

Z1	**= HRmax - 80 to 70 (recovery)**
Z1-2	**= HRmax - 65 (warm-up)**
Z2	**= HRmax - 60 to 50 (endurance)**
Z2-3	**= HRmax - 45 ***
Z3	**= HRmax - 40 to 30 ***
Z3-4	**= HRmax - 25 (race)**
Z4	**= HRmax - 20 to 0 (sprint)**

Example for a person with a maximum heart rate of 180 (HRmax=180).

This could for instance be a typical 40 year old runner. The approximation for age is HRmax=220-age. For this example, HRmax=220-40=**180**.

Z1-2 Run HR at around **115** (HRmax-65)

Z2 Run HR kept below **130** (HRmax-50)

Z3-4 Run is mostly with HR at around **155** (HRmax-25) with last mile at **170** (HRmax-10)

Z2-4 Run is mostly with HR at around **120 to 130** (HRmax-60to50) with last mile at **170** (HRmax-10)

Please Note These 16-week Training Plans are for runners aged from 18 years to 75 years. These are based on the the assumption that the maximum heart rate (HRmax) will be 220 minus age (in years).

In fact, there is considerable variation in HRmax at any given age. Therefore, a 50 year old may have the same HRmax as the average 40 year old (180 beats per minute), so this individual should follow the training plan with the HR's for the average 40 year old.

It may be better to remove age from the discussion completely. This is because:

• Age in itself is not a limiter on performance. You can keep improving your marathon times as you age.

• To chose your Marathon Training Plan and your Marathon Raceday Plan, you just need to know your HRmax and your Target Marathon Finish time. Age does not actually have anything to do with it.

• If your HRmax is significantly different than average for your age then you should follow the plans that are correct for your HRmax (rather than age).

Zones 1-4 Heart Rate (HR)

for runners with HRmax in range 200 - 175

(typically these runners are aged 18 - 45)

HRmax (average for age)	200 b p m 18-20y	195 b p m 25y	190 b p m 30y	185 b p m 35y	180 b p m 40y	175 b p m 45
Z 1 = HRmax -80to70	120 - 130	115 - 125	110 - 120	105 - 115	100 - 110	9 5 - 105
Z 1-2 = HRmax-65	135	130	125	120	115	110
Z 2 = HRmax -60to50	140 - 150	135 - 145	130 - 140	125 - 135	120 - 130	115 - 125
Z 2-3 = HRmax-45	155	150	145	140	135	130
Z 3 = HRmax -40to30	160 - 170	155 - 165	150 - 160	145 - 155	140 - 150	135 - 145
Z 3-4 = HRmax-25	175	170	165	160	155	150
Z 4 = HRmax -20to0	180 - 200	175 - 195	170 - 190	165 - 185	160 - 180	155 - 175

Zones 1-4 Heart Rate (HR)

for runners with HRmax in range 170 to 145

(typically these runners are aged 50 - 75)

HRmax (average for age)	170 b p m (50y)	165 b p m (55y)	160 b p m (60y)	155 b p m (65y)	150 b p m (70y)	145 b p m (75y)
Z 1 = HRmax -80to70	90 - 100	8 5 - 95	8 0 - 90	7 5 - 85	7 0 - 80	6 5 - 75
Z1-2 = HRmax-65	105	100	95	90	85	80
Z 2 = HRmax -60to50	1 1 0 - 120	105 - 115	100 - 110	9 5 - 105	9 0 - 100	8 5 - 95
Z2-3 = HRmax-45	125	120	115	110	105	100
Z 3 = HRmax -40to30	1 3 0 - 140	125 - 135	120 - 130	115 - 125	110 - 120	105 - 115
Z3-4 = HRmax-25	145	140	135	130	125	120
Z 4 = HRmax -20to0	1 5 0 - 170	145 - 165	140 - 160	135 - 155	130 - 150	125 - 145

Marathon Training Schedules

The 24 Mile Peak Week Marathon Training Schedule is in Table 1.

This is probably the minimum running miles that can be done in training in order to prepare adequately to race a marathon.

There are only 11 running miles in total for the first of the 16 weeks. The 11 miles are made up of 2 short runs of 3 miles each (**Intervals** and **Tempo**) plus one **Long Run** of 5 miles.

For this schedule, the short runs do not increase in mileage but they stay at 3 miles for the whole of the 16 weeks. These short runs help develop speed and help raise the lactate threshold. They don't need to be long runs to be effective.

The once weekly long run increases by one mile each week, until reaching a maximum of 18 miles (3 weeks before the marathon race).

In my view, everyone needs to do at least one long run of at least 18 miles before attempting the 26.2 miles of a marathon.

The body needs to become tolerant and adapted to the endurance required for several hours of running.

This schedule has just 3 running days each week and there is never running on consecutive days. Following the one long run each week, there are always 2 days away from running.

Who would chose the training schedule with the minimum of running miles shown in Table 1?

This training schedule could be appropriate for somebody who's body cannot tolerate too much running because of a tendency to injury. If this is the case and time is not a limiter, then they should do lots of swimming and cycling on non-running days and on running days if possible; in order to increase fitness and endurance.

Also this schedule might be chosen by somebody who simply does not have enough time in their busy life to be able to do more running. It would therefore be a good investment of precious time to complete this minimum training schedule as it represents the most efficient preparation needed to reach the marathon finish line safely and enjoyably.

Tempo, Intervals, RnR, Z1-2, Z2, Z3, Z2-4 are
explained on pages 148-151

Table 1. Dr Jim's Marathon Training Schedule - 24 Mile Peak

	Mon	Tue	Wed	Thur	Fri	Sat	Sun	Total
1	RnR	RnR	3mile Z1-2	RnR	3mile Z1-2	RnR	5mile Z1-2	11mile
2	RnR	RnR	3mile Z1-2	RnR	3mile Z1-2	RnR	6mile Z1-2	12mile
3	RnR	RnR	3mile Z1-2	RnR	3mile Z1-2	RnR	7mile Z1-2	13mile
4	RnR	RnR	3mile Z1-2	RnR	3mile Z1-2	RnR	8mile Z1-2	14mile
5	RnR	RnR	3mile Z2	RnR	3mile Z2	RnR	9mile Z1-2	15mile
6	RnR	RnR	3mile Interv	RnR	3mile Tempo	RnR	10mile Z1-2	16mile
7	RnR	RnR	3mile Interv	RnR	3mile Tempo	RnR	11mile Z1-2	17mile
8	RnR	RnR	3mile Interv	RnR	3mile Tempo	RnR	12mile Z1-2	18mile
9	RnR	RnR	3mile Interv	RnR	3mile Tempo	RnR	**13mile HM**	19mile
10	RnR	RnR	3mile Interv	RnR	3mile Tempo	RnR	15mile Z2-4	21mile
11	RnR	RnR	3mile Interv	RnR	3mile Tempo	RnR	16mile Z2-4	22mile
12	RnR	RnR	3mile Interv	RnR	3mile Tempo	RnR	17mile Z2-4	23mile
13	RnR	RnR	3mile Interv	RnR	3mile Tempo	RnR	18mile Z2-4	24mile
14	RnR	RnR	3mile Interv	RnR	3mile Tempo	RnR	13mile Z2-4	19mile
15	RnR	RnR	3mile Interv	RnR	3mile Tempo	RnR	10mile Z2-4	16mile
16	RnR	3mile Z3	RnR	2mile Z2	RnR	**REST**	**26mile M**	31mile

The 32 Mile Peak Week Marathon Training Schedule is in Table 1A.

Who is this schedule for?

This schedule would be ideal for a large proportion of people because it provides good marathon preparation that is more than just the minimum training requirement. However, it is not a high mileage schedule.

Tempo, Intervals, RnR, Z1-2, Z2, Z3, Z2-4 are explained on pages 148-151

Table 1A. Dr Jim's Marathon Training Schedule - 32 Mile Peak Week

	Mon	Tue	Wed	Thur	Fri	Sat	Sun	Total
1	RnR	RnR	4mile Z1-2	RnR	4mile Z1-2	RnR	6mile Z1-2	14mile
2	RnR	RnR	5mile Z1-2	RnR	5mile Z1-2	RnR	6mile Z1-2	16mile
3	RnR	RnR	6mile Z1-2	RnR	6mile Z1-2	RnR	7mile Z1-2	19mile
4	RnR	RnR	6mile Z1-2	RnR	6mile Z1-2	RnR	8mile Z1-2	20mile
5	RnR	RnR	6mile Z2	RnR	6mile Z2	RnR	9mile Z1-2	21mile
6	RnR	RnR	6mile Interv	RnR	6mile Tempo	RnR	10mile Z1-2	22mile
7	RnR	RnR	6mile Interv	RnR	6mile Tempo	RnR	11mile Z1-2	23mile
8	RnR	RnR	6mile Interv	RnR	6mile Tempo	RnR	12mile Z1-2	24mile
9	RnR	RnR	6mile Interv	RnR	4mile Tempo	RnR	13mile HM	23mile
10	RnR	RnR	6mile Interv	RnR	6mile Tempo	RnR	15mile Z2-4	27mile
11	RnR	RnR	6mile Interv	RnR	6mile Tempo	RnR	16mile Z2-4	28mile
12	RnR	RnR	6mile Interv	RnR	6mile Tempo	RnR	18mile Z2-4	30mile
13	RnR	RnR	6mile Interv	RnR	6mile Tempo	RnR	20mile Z2-4	32mile
14	RnR	RnR	5mile Interv	RnR	5mile Tempo	RnR	15mile Z2-4	25mile
15	RnR	RnR	4mile Interv	RnR	4mile Tempo	RnR	12mile Z2-4	20mile
16	RnR	3mile Z3	RnR	2mile Z2	RnR	REST	26mile M	31mile

The 40 Mile Peak Week Marathon Training Schedule is in Table 2.

The 50 Mile Peak Week Marathon Training Schedule is in Table 2A.

The 60 Mile Peak Week Marathon Training Schedule is in Table 3.

These schedules have 4 running days each week. They follow the same principles as the 24 Mile Peak Week Schedule, but the mileages are higher and an extra (low intensity **Z2 run**) occurs on the day before the long run.

Each week there are 3 days off running and each of these days follow high intensity days or the long run day. These non-running days are good for achieving recovery in time for the next important running day.

Being too fatigued at the start of a high intensity running session will reduce the performance gains that we are aiming for.

Who are these schedules for?
Many successful and serious marathon runners do running training mileages in this range. Nearly all my marathon training has been related to these schedules.

Tempo, Intervals, RnR, Z1-2, Z2, Z3, Z2-4 are explained on pages 148-151

Table 2. Dr Jim's Marathon Training Schedule - 40 Mile Peak Week

	Mon	Tue	Wed	Thur	Fri	Sat	Sun	Total
1	RnR	3mile Z1-2	RnR	3mile Z1-2	RnR	3mile Z1-2	6mile Z1-2	15mile
2	RnR	4mile Z1-2	RnR	4mile Z1-2	RnR	4mile Z1-2	10mile Z1-2	22mile
3	RnR	5mile Z2	RnR	5mile Z2	RnR	5mile Z2	12mile Z1-2	27mile
4	RnR	6mile Z2	RnR	6mile Z2	RnR	6mile Z2	14mile Z1-2	32mile
5	RnR	6mile Interval	RnR	6mile Tempo	RnR	6mile Z2	15mile Z1-2	33mile
6	RnR	6mile Interval	RnR	6mile Tempo	RnR	6mile Z2	16mile Z1-2	34mile
7	RnR	6mile Interval	RnR	6mile Tempo	RnR	6mile Z2	17mile Z1-2	35mile
8	RnR	6mile Interval	RnR	6mile Tempo	RnR	6mile Z2	18mile Z1-2	36mile
9	RnR	5mile Interval	RnR	5mile Tempo	RnR	3mile Z1-2	**13mile HM Z3-4**	26mile
10	RnR	6mile Interval	RnR	6mile Tempo	RnR	6mile Z2	15mile Z2-4	33mile
11	RnR	6mile Interval	RnR	6mile Tempo	RnR	6mile Z2	18mile Z2-4	36mile
12	RnR	6mile Interval	RnR	6mile Tempo	RnR	6mile Z2	20mile Z2-4	38mile
13	RnR	6mile Interval	RnR	6mile Tempo	RnR	6mile Z2	22mile Z2-4	40mile
14	RnR	5mile Interval	RnR	5mile Tempo	RnR	5mile Z2	18mile Z2-4	33mile
15	RnR	4mile Interval	RnR	4mile Tempo	RnR	4mile Z2	13mile Z2-4	25mile
16	RnR	3mile Z3	RnR	3mile Z2	RnR	**REST**	**26mile M**	32mile

Table 2A. Dr Jim's Marathon Training Schedule - 50 Mile Peak Week

	Mon	Tue	Wed	Thur	Fri	Sat	Sun	Total
1	RnR	4mile Z1-2	RnR	4mile Z1-2	RnR	4mile Z1-2	10mile Z1-2	22mile
2	RnR	5mile Z1-2	RnR	5mile Z1-2	RnR	5mile Z1-2	12mile Z1-2	27mile
3	RnR	6mile Z2	RnR	6mile Z2	RnR	6mile Z2	13mile Z1-2	31mile
4	RnR	6mile Z2	RnR	6mile Z2	RnR	6mile Z2	14mile Z1-2	32mile
5	RnR	7mile Interva	RnR	7mile Tempo	RnR	6mile Z2	15mile Z1-2	35mile
6	RnR	7mile Interva	RnR	8mile Tempo	RnR	6mile Z2	16mile Z1-2	37mile
7	RnR	7mile Interva	RnR	8mile Tempo	RnR	6mile Z2	17mile Z1-2	38mile
8	RnR	7mile Interva	RnR	8mile Tempo	RnR	6mile Z2	18mile Z1-2	39mile
9	RnR	7mile Interva	RnR	8mile Tempo	RnR	3mile Z1-2	**13mile HM**	31mile
10	RnR	6mile Interva	RnR	10mile Tempo	RnR	6mile Z2	18mile Z2-4	40mile
11	RnR	6mile Interva	RnR	13mile Tempo	RnR	6mile Z2	20mile Z2-4	45mile
12	RnR	7mile Interva	RnR	14mile Tempo	RnR	6mile Z2	21mile Z2-4	48mile
13	RnR	7mile Interva	RnR	15mile Tempo	RnR	6mile Z2	22mile Z2-4	50mile
14	RnR	6mile Interva	RnR	8mile Tempo	RnR	5mile Z2	18mile Z2-4	37mile
15	RnR	5mile Interva	RnR	5mile Tempo	RnR	5mile Z2	13mile Z2-4	28mile
16	RnR	3mile Z3	RnR	3mile Z2	RnR	**REST**	**26mile M**	32mile

Table 3. Dr Jim's Marathon Training Schedule - 60 Mile Peak Week

	Mon	Tue	Wed	Thur	Fri	Sat	Sun	Total
1	RnR	4mile Z1-2	RnR	4mile Z1-2	RnR	4mile Z1-2	10mile Z1-2	22mile
2	RnR	5mile Z1-2	RnR	5mile Z1-2	RnR	5mile Z2	12mile Z1-2	27mile
3	RnR	6mile Z2	RnR	6mile Z2	RnR	6mile Z2	15mile Z1-2	33mile
4	RnR	6mile Z2	RnR	6mile Z2	RnR	6mile Z2	18mile Z1-2	36mile
5	RnR	7mile Interval	RnR	7mile Tempo	RnR	7mile Z2	18mile Z1-2	39mile
6	RnR	7mile Interval	RnR	10mile Tempo	RnR	7mile Z2	20mile Z1-2	44mile
7	RnR	7mile Interval	RnR	12mile Tempo	RnR	7mile Z2	20mile Z1-2	46mile
8	RnR	8mile Interval	RnR	12mile Tempo	RnR	8mile Z2	20mile Z1-2	48mile
9	RnR	8mile Interval	RnR	10mile Tempo	RnR	6mile Z1-2	**13mile HM Z3-4**	37mile
10	RnR	10mile Interval	RnR	12mile Tempo	RnR	8mile Z2	15mile Z2-4	45mile
11	RnR	10mile Interval	RnR	15mile Tempo	RnR	10mile Z2	18mile Z2-4	53mile
12	RnR	10mile Interval	RnR	16mile Tempo	RnR	11mile Z2	20mile Z2-4	57mile
13	RnR	10mile Interval	RnR	17mile Tempo	RnR	11mile Z2	22mile Z2-4	60mile
14	RnR	7mile Interval	RnR	7mile Tempo	RnR	7mile Z2	18mile Z2-4	39mile
15	RnR	5mile Interval	RnR	5mile Tempo	RnR	5mile Z2	13mile Z2-4	28mile
16	RnR	3mile Z3	RnR	3mile Z2	RnR	**REST**	**26mile M**	32mile

I do long runs with two 750ml drink bottles in a running waist belt.

This can be supplemented with a 500ml bottle in the hand plus money to buy isotonic drinks if need be. The pouch is for food, mobile phone and a bin-bag as emergency extra clothing. Carry ID plus next-of-kin address and phone number.

More drink is needed for longer distances or in hot weather, so plan route around shops or where water is available. If water is unavailable on the route, run short loops from home or car (with water in the car).
Wear high visibility clothing and lights after sunset.

The 80 Mile Peak Week Marathon Training Schedule is in Table 4.

The 100 Mile Peak Week Marathon Training Schedule is in Table 5.

Both these schedules have 4 running days each week for the first month, but after that there are 6 running days each week. They follow the same principles of the lower mileage volume Training Schedules, with 3 key types of run (**Intervals, Tempo** and **Long**) but the mileages for each run are greater. In addition there are up to 3 extra running days each week that are mostly at **Z2**.

Most runners find that their performances do steadily improve with increased weekly training running mileage, so long as there is a good balance of types of run (as outlined in these schedules). My current PB was achieved using the schedule in Table 4.

These high volume running schedules are only possible if runners remain free of injury. If injury, strain or inflammation occur then it is best to switch to a lower mileage schedule that has more non-running days.

Tempo, Intervals, RnR, Z1-2, Z2, Z3, Z2-4 are explained on pages 148-151

Table 4. Dr Jim's Marathon Training Schedule - 80 Mile Peak Week

	Mon	Tue	Wed	Thur	Fri	Sat	Sun	Total
1	RnR	5mile Z1-2	RnR	5mile Z1-2	RnR	5mile Z1-2	12mile Z1-2	27mile
2	RnR	6mile Z1-2	RnR	6mile Z1-2	RnR	6mile Z2	15mile Z1-2	33mile
3	RnR	6mile Z2	RnR	6mile Z2	RnR	6mile Z2	15mile Z1-2	33mile
4	RnR	6mile Z2	RnR	6mile Z2	RnR	6mile Z2	18mile Z1-2	36mile
5	RnR	7mile Interval	3mile Z2	7mile Tempo	3mile Z2	7mile Z2	18mile Z1-2	45mile
6	RnR	7mile Interval	3mile Z2	10mile Tempo	3mile Z2	7mile Z2	20mile Z1-2	50mile
7	RnR	7mile Interval	4mile Z2	12mile Tempo	4mile Z2	7mile Z2	20mile Z1-2	54mile
8	RnR	8mile Interval	5mile Z2	12mile Tempo	5mile Z2	8mile Z2	20mile Z1-2	58mile
9	RnR	8mile Interval	5mile Z2	10mile Tempo	5mile Z2	6mile Z1-2	**13mile HM Z3-4**	47mile
10	RnR	10mile Interval	6mile Z2	12mile Tempo	6mile Z2	8mile Z2	15mile Z2-4	57mile
11	RnR	10mile Interval	6mile Z2	15mile Tempo	6mile Z2	10mile Z2	19mile Z2-4	66mile
12	RnR	11mile Interval	7mile Z2	17mile Tempo	7mile Z2	12mile Z2	21mile Z2-4	75mile
13	RnR	11mile Interval	8mile Z2	18mile Tempo	8mile Z2	13mile Z2	22mile Z2-4	80mile
14	RnR	8mile Interval	5mile Z2	12mile Tempo	5mile Z2	9mile Z2	18mile Z2-4	57mile
15	RnR	5mile Interval	4mile Z2	5mile Tempo	4mile Z2	5mile Z2	13mile Z2-4	36mile
16	RnR	3mile Z3	RnR	3mile Z2	RnR	**REST**	**26mile M**	32mile

Table 5. Dr Jim's Marathon Training Schedule - 100 Mile Peak Week

	Mon	Tue	Wed	Thur	Fri	Sat	Sun	Total
1	RnR	5mile Z1-2	5mile Z2	5mile Z1-2	5mile Z2	5mile Z1-2	12mile Z1-2	37mile
2	RnR	6mile Z1-2	5mile Z2	6mile Z1-2	5mile Z2	6mile Z2	15mile Z1-2	43mile
3	RnR	6mile Z2	5mile Z2	6mile Z2	5mile Z2	6mile Z2	18mile Z1-2	46mile
4	RnR	7mile Z2	5mile Z2	7mile Z2	5mile Z2	7mile Z2	18mile Z1-2	49mile
5	RnR	7mile Interval	6mile Z2	9mile Tempo	6mile Z2	7mile Z2	20mile Z1-2	55mile
6	RnR	8mile Interval	8mile Z2	10mile Tempo	8mile Z2	8mile Z2	20mile Z1-2	62mile
7	RnR	9mile Interval	9mile Z2	12mile Tempo	10mile Z2	8mile Z2	20mile Z1-2	68mile
8	RnR	10mile Interval	10mile Z2	12mile Tempo	10mile Z2	10mile Z2	20mile Z1-2	72mile
9	RnR	10mile Interval	10mile Z2	12mile Tempo	5mile Z2	5mile Z1-2	**13mile HM Z3-4**	55mile
10	RnR	10mile Interval	14mile Z2	12mile Tempo	16mile Z2	14mile Z2	18mile Z2-4	84mile
11	RnR	10mile Interval	16mile Z2	15mile Tempo	18mile Z2	14mile Z2	20mile Z2-4	93mile
12	RnR	10mile Interval	17mile Z2	16mile Tempo	18mile Z2	15mile Z2	21mile Z2-4	97mile
13	RnR	11mile Interval	18mile Z2	16mile Tempo	18mile Z2	15mile Z2	22mile Z2-4	100mile
14	RnR	8mile Interval	12mile Z2	12mile Tempo	5mile Z2	9mile Z2	20mile Z2-4	66mile
15	RnR	5mile Interval	4mile Z2	10mile Tempo	4mile Z2	5mile Z2	13mile Z2-4	41mile
16	RnR	3mile Z3	RnR	3mile Z2	RnR	**REST**	**26mile M**	32mile

164

CHAPTER 16

Triathlon

Those of you who are not currently triathletes, please do give triathlon a try, because it will be great fun and can boost your general fitness. The swimming and cycling provide opportunities for increased training without leading to overuse running injuries.

Many people find that their standalone marathon finish times improve once they have taken to doing iron-distance triathlons.

The endurance gains from iron-distance triathlon training takes you to a new level, after which a 26.2 mile run on its own seems somewhat easier.

Do not worry if your swimming is poor or very poor, because you can wear a wetsuit. A wetsuit allows you to just float and paddle. This is how I started in 2008 and swimming gradually improved to 'average' level by 2012.

Race Report:
Dr Jim's Ironman Barcelona 2015

Pre-Race

A 140.6 full-distance 100% effort 3 weeks earlier at Challenge Weymouth, followed by an 80% effort at Gauntlet 70.3 middle-distance 1 week prior to Barcelona.

Race Day

Perfect conditions with calm sea and 20 degrees air temperature with no rain and neither wind nor sunshine.

Swim:

The rolling-start to the swim made a stress-free experience and it was easy to find correctly paced swimmers to draft off. Exited the water in 1:18, which was 2 minutes slower than Personal Best (PB).

Cycle:

Being a relatively poor swimmer, I was very far back from the leaders when I started cycling. I overtook more than a thousand riders during the 112 miles and only 2 or 3 riders overtook me.

Lots of riders in front causes obstruction and delays on tricky technical courses. On the wide flat roads at Barcelona, the constant need to overtake other riders was a bonus, because there is a small perfectly legal drafting benefit for the few seconds that each overtaking manoeuvre requires.

I decided to give it 100% and try for a first ever sub-5 hour ironman cycle on this fast course. I was not thinking about the run at this stage.

There was no need to stop for toilet or for fuel, with the perfectly judged supply of 3 litres of fluid that I was carrying (15 gels, 3 salt tablets and 4 sachets of isotonic dissolved in the drinks system).

The plan worked well and I completed the cycle in 4:49. This was a massive personal best for a cycle within an iron-distance triathlon. The average cycle speed was 37.34 kph!

Run:

My run started with gut ache and indigestion so I did not take a gel for the first 40 minutes. I was happy with the cycle and not too bothered about doing a great run, so I started slowly. My gut began to feel good after the first hour, so I focused on trying to get a sub-10 hour finish.

I got the maths wrong by a 15 minute margin and sprinted frantically for the last 2 miles in order to squeeze in under 10 hours. In fact I managed to run a 3:32 marathon, which was only 6 minutes slower than my iron-run PB.

Post-Race

I felt fantastic and immediately ate a big Spanish meal, including 3 beers. I usually feel exhausted and nauseous after iron-distance races, so this was a pleasant surprise.

The **9:45 finish time** was a massive PB and a cause for great celebration. I would never normally drink more than one alcoholic drink straight after a marathon or long distance triathlon. This was special.

There are many things that can go wrong with a race of this duration and I have had plenty of poor results to prove it. Everything went well on this occasion. The gut problems at the start of the run probably helped with run pacing, as I was forced to start slowly and build up pace gradually.

Dr Jim's Iron-Distance Triathlon Tips

If you are a triathlete who is looking for Dr Jim's tips for getting faster at iron-distance racing and perhaps getting to Kona, here they are:

1. Whatever your swimming ability, keep a regular schedule of 3 swims each week. More than 3 is great, but never do less than 2 swims in a week.

Pay attention to form and drills plus a mix of endurance and speed swim sets. This book will not go into detail on swimming training.

Suffice is to say that the iron-distance finish time gains from improved swimming are rather small compared to cycling and running.

2. Count your weekly cycling hours and build this to a peak 2-3 weeks before the iron-distance race. You cannot do too many cycling miles, so long as you build up the mileage gradually and do a 2-3 week taper before the iron-distance race. More miles the better.

3. Cycle to work and cycle to the swimming pool. Do long distance cycling into the countryside at weekends with your friends. Sprint up some hills from time to time but 90% of the cycling miles will be in Heart Rate Zone 2.

4. Cycle whilst watching movies, training videos and television by setting up a home trainer and a fan. Use a power meter and observe your wattage rise as you 'build a bigger engine'.

5. Do a 25 mile cycling time trial or a Standard (Olympic) Distance Triathlon about a month before the iron-distance race. Aim for a maximum effort cycle and get as near to 25mph average speed as you can (especially if the course is flat and there is no traffic).

6. Enter an iron-distance race that has a flat non-technical cycle course (such as Florida or Barcelona) if you are not principally a cyclist. This way the bike ride will be a test of fitness rather than a test of cycling skills.

7. Do all the marathon running training as detailed in this book already. Because you will be doing lots of swimming and cycling, it will be best to chose a plan with just 40 to 60 maximum running miles in a week.

8. Always do your running after a cycle whenever possible. Even a short cycle for 10 minutes is useful as a warm-up as well as adapting to running when coming off the bike. Do at least one century ride (100 miles of cycling) and make sure you go for a run straight afterwards with a quick transition.

9. Aim to do the iron-run at around 30 minutes slower than your standalone marathon time. A good iron-run will separate you from everyone else. There are large gains, in terms of iron-distance finish time, to be had from a good run. The best swimmers can gain

20 minutes on the average swimmers, but best runners can gain 60 minutes on the average runners.

10. The most important priority is to have a very long training day, once each week, that preferably involves all 3 disciplines.

This must be the priority because you want your body to adapt to 6, 7, 8, 9 or even 10 hours training in one day. These very long training days are in Heart Rate Zone 1-2.

This all-day training session gets gradually longer each week until peaking (2-3 weeks before the iron-distance race) at 9 or 10 hours. On race day, you will consider the 140.6 miles to be just part of your normal routine.

11. Do lots of iron-distance races (if you can afford the registration fees) or do numerous 140.6 mile training days in your own neighbourhood. Your body will adapt to the endurance demanded from this mileage and your iron-distance ability will steadily improve . Keep at it and don't let those endurance adaptations leak away from underuse.

12. The nutrition plan for these long periods of exercise will be perfected by trial and error. Adapt to using fat as a fuel in training (by snacking on cheese and nuts for example). Take plenty of salt. Avoid routinely consuming glucose in gels and drinks in training. Use glucose on race days.

13. Do not assume that it will be easier as you get older to qualify for the Ironman Triathlon World Championship in Kona, Hawaii. The better athletes keep competing as they get older and age doesn't seem to slow the best ones down very much. There seems to be a higher proportion of relatively slower triathletes in the younger age-groups and those age-groups have a larger number of Kona slots available to them. Don't delay or put it off. Go for it now!

CHAPTER 17

Recipes

These recipes are good for Dr Jim but you should consult your physician before changing your diet.

A terrific nurse, who I work with, has transformed her own life with the LCHF diet and transformed the lives of many patients with her LCHF dietary advice (particularly for diabetics).

We routinely discuss what we are having for lunch and enjoy talking about food in general. We are gradually converting the rest of the workforce over to our way of thinking. Here are few things that we like.

LCHF Brownies

It was fun doing this baking with my 15 year old son, who got quite interested in the chemistry of baking soda as well as eating the product.

These can be more of a savoury than a cake. I eat these with cream and fruit if I want a dessert. I have also eaten these LCHF Brownies with cheese for lunch. You get a long-lasting energy release with this kind of food rather than the usual sugar-rush from traditional cakes. The small amount of carbohydrate content is mostly from the goji berry and the tiny proportion of sugar in the cooking chocolate (70 - 85% cocoa).

The cocoa has some bitterness that stops them being too 'more-ish', so maybe that bitterness is in fact a good thing for those trying to reduce body-weight. If your first batch of these Brownies are too bitter for you, I advise increasing the desiccated coconut content and reducing the amount of cooking chocolate.

Ingredients for LCHF Brownies:
1/4 cup of Ground Almonds

1/4 cup of Desiccated Coconut

1/8 cup of Ground Flax Seed

1/4 cup of Mixed Chopped Nuts

1/4 cup of Mixed Seeds (Chia, Sunflower, Pumpkin, Sesame etc)

Pinch of Salt

3 Beaten Eggs

1 teaspoon (5ml) Vanilla Essence

1/2 teaspoon (2.5ml) Baking Soda

1/4 cup Melted Butter or Coconut oil

1/8 cup of Goji Berries

50-100g (between half a bar and a whole bar) of Cooking Chocolate

Method for LCHF Brownies:

Melt the butter and chocolate at low heat in a large frying pan.

Thoroughly mix in all the other ingredients.

Evenly distribute the mixture in an oiled baking tray (or fill a dozen or so cake cases and place those on the baking tray).

Bake in an oven at 180 celsius (360 F) for 15 to 20 minutes.

LCHF porridge

Ingredients for LCHF porridge:

Porridge oats are over 60% carbohydrate (8% fat, 11% protein), therefore I replace the majority of the porridge oats with LCHF alternatives listed below:

Ground Almonds (56% fat, 26.5% protein, 6.0% carbs)
Desiccated Coconut (62% fat, 5.5% protein, 6.5% carbs)
Chia Seeds (60% fat, 26.5% protein, 6% carbs)
Sesame Seeds (58% fat, 21.5% protein, 1% carbs)
Ground Flax Seed (42% fat, 18% protein, 1.5% carbs)
Sunflower Seeds (51.5% fat, 21% protein, 11.5% carbs)
Linseed (62% fat, 5.6% protein, 6.4% carbs)
Pumpkin Seeds (42% fat, 18.5% protein, 1.5% carbs)
Whole Walnuts (65% fat, 15% protein, 7% carbs)
Dried Goji Berries (2% fat, 14% protein, 70% carbs)
Fresh Blueberries (1% fat, 4% protein, 70% carbs)
Full fat milk (4% fat, 3.5% protein, 5% carbs)
Double cream (50.5% fat, 1.5% protein, 1.5% carbs)

As this is high energy food, my portion is just one third of the volume of regular porridge. About one spoonful of each of the main ingredients is enough.

Method for LCHF porridge:

Evenly mix all the ingredients except the cream and blueberries, then microwave at full power for between 50 seconds and 90 seconds (depending on the size of the porridge portion). Put the the cream and blueberries on the top after the porridge has been heated.

The goji berries and blueberries are high in carbohydrate but they make up only a small proportion of the ingredients. These berries provide vitamins and some sweetness that helps make the porridge taste delicious.

I eat a small bowl of this porridge every morning at around 0630 and I don't feel hungry again until 1230.

Mashed Cauliflower with Cream Cheese

This is a great alternative to mashed potato. A similar idea is to use coarsely mashed cauliflower as an alternative to rice.

Cauliflower pizza

My daughter makes delicious pizzas using baked mashed cauliflower instead of a normal (flour) pizza base.

Courgetti (also known as Spiralized Zucchini)

This is a delicious alternative to pasta.

Raw vegetables instead of biscuits or potato chips

Celery and peppers are great to have with cheese or hummus.

Eat lots of (above ground) vegetables

Routinely apply an olive oil dressing.

Less fruit

Most fruits (avocado is an exception) have very high sugar content. There is as much sugar in orange juice as there is in cola. Have fruit as a treat (maybe one portion each day). Eat avocado or raw vegetables as an alternative to fruits that have high sugar content.

Enjoy your food

These are just a few things that I like to eat. However, there is a whole world of other food for you to explore. For instance, take a look at:
https://www.dietdoctor.com/low-carb/recipes

Food is one of life's great pleasures and foods rich in healthy natural oils tend to be delicious. Aim to have a minimum of 60% of your food energy intake from fat/oil.

Explore what is available in your local stores and try lots of different things. Usually the packaging will state the percentages of fat, protein and carbohydrate.

Sometimes you will have a meal or a snack that does not conform to the advised ratios, and that is alright but make this the exception and not the norm.

Increase your dietary fat to 70+% at times when you are seriously getting lean, fit and most adapted to endurance exercise.

I eat what is in the LCHF column in the table below.

	low fat diet	LCHF	high protein diet
Fat %	20	60-70	15
Protein %	20	20	70
Carbs %	60	10-20	15

Avoid Beers (except Lite) and Ales

Beer has a lot of 'hidden sugar' in the form of carbohydrates such as maltose. It would be good for most people to drink less alcohol.

It is important to have celebrations and when we do consume alcoholic beverages it is better to drink lower carbohydrate options, for example:

Whiskey/Bourbon and Soda
Rum and Diet Cola
Gin and Diet Tonic
Dry Wine
Lite Beer

Section C

"Go"

CHAPTER 18

Pre-Race Strategy

You should have plenty of rest on the day before your big race.

In the words of Benjamin Franklin "by failing to prepare, you are preparing to fail". Let's not do that.

One benefit from participating in lots of races is that we find out what works best for us and that is often by 'trial and error'.

Race week

Follow the training plan in this book that is most suitable for you. Do some low volume low intensity training during the the first few days of race week. It is too late to make any fitness gains, but do this light training to avoid losing fitness.

Get to the race venue a couple of days before the race (unless it is in your home town). It is good to settle-in so that you can get organised then have a relaxed day before the race.

Try to get accommodation within easy reach of the race start to save energy on race day. A one mile gentle warm-up jog to the start on race morning would be ideal, but it is not always possible to find somewhere to stay that is this close.

Aim to attend the expo and collect your race pack 2 days before the race, so you can totally rest on the day before the race.

Study the route to the race start and arrange your transport. Carefully consider the other options if you are not staying close enough to the start to be able to walk or jog there. Chat to other guests if you are staying at a hotel, because you may be able to share a taxi.

Eat a low-fibre high carbohydrate diet for the final 24 hours as it is best to race on an empty colon. White rice is good. Enjoy some chocolate. This is a low residue diet.

Spend the day before the race preparing your kit and visualising the things that will happen on race-day. This includes every tiny detail (such as breakfast, dressing, toilet, clothing for journey to start etc).

Write a list of all these important things to be done for race day, then you will sleep safe in the knowledge that you cannot forget anything so you can "turn your brain off" overnight.

Put strict limits on social media at this stage, but acknowledge the support of well-wishers. Prioritise getting kit prepared and having a good sleep.

Get to bed early and aim for 8 hours sleep then get up early. Avoid any sedatives, alcohol or painkillers. Do take any regular medication that has been advised or prescribed by your physician (doctor) but take nothing else.

Race Day

You have slept well and got every tiny detail of race day mapped out in your head (as well as written down).

You have studied the route to the start and arranged your transport, so you know exactly what to do and when. You will not be late and you will not get stressed or rushed as a result. It is always better to arrive early and get to the race toilets before the queue is massive.

Breakfast is crucial and you consume things that you are familiar with. My custom is to eat rice pudding because it is high carb but low fibre (and it will be fully digested within an hour or so). I always have one cup of coffee at around this time.

Take with you a few gels and a bottle of energy drink to consume in the last couple of hours between leaving your hotel and the starting-gun going off.

I carry 3 salt tablets and 6 energy gels with me to consume during the run. If there is a drinks station at every mile of the race, then I do not run with a drink bottle. If the the drinks stations are not located at each mile, then I carry a small drink bottle in the rear pocket of my triathlon vest.

Have a strategy for shoe issues (getting a stone inside the shoe or a shoelace coming undone). I use triathlon elasticated laces in my running shoes, so it is easy to rapidly remove a stone then put the shoe back on. Triathlon laces do not come undone. You do not want a shoelace problem during the race, as it disturbs your rhythm as well as wasting precious time.

I race with a chest strap heart rate monitor (HRM) and a GPS watch for pacing. I memorise my mile-by-mile race plan and it is written down so that I can read it again shortly before the race starts.

Do not forget suncream and lubrication.

Recognise your 'race-day nerves' for what they are and avoid getting into arguments or fussing over unimportant things. Use this nervousness constructively by channeling this energy into running power during the race. Do not expend energy in unhelpful ways by getting flustered.

You have warmed-up many times before and you know what to do instinctively. It takes 10-20 minutes to raise the body temperature 0.5 C for optimum running efficiency. Do the warm-up with the minimum of energy expended (low heart rate).

Do some gentle walking lunges once fully warmed up. Wear a disposable bin-liner or some clothing that you will discard shortly before the gun goes off.

Seed yourself correctly in the starting pen so that you are alongside runners who will run at your pace.

Good luck and have a safe successful race!

CHAPTER 19

Calculating Target Marathon Pace and Target Marathon Finish Time

It is important to pick a Target Marathon Finish Time that is optimal for our current level of fitness and marathon running ability.

If we run slower than our optimal pace then we will finish slower than our potential for that day. If we try to run faster than the optimal pace then we will fatigue early and finish slower than our potential for that day.

A well paced marathon will have 'even splits' and this means that the first 13.1 miles will be completed in the same time as the second 13.1 miles. Ideally, the second 13.1 miles will be about a minute faster than the first 13.1 miles. If there is more than 3 minutes difference between the first and second half of the marathon, then you did not get the pacing right.

I have done a survey of half-marathon and full-marathon finish times from local athletes with a wide range of ages and abilities. These half-marathon and full-marathon race results were at the same fitness level for each individual athlete, in order to find the relationship between performances at the two distances.

A remarkably linear relationship was found between performances for each athlete at the two distances. That means that for all levels of ability, we can predict quite accurately how fast an individual should be able to run a marathon when we know how fast that individual ran a half-marathon.

Results from Mo Farah (Olympic 5k and 10k Gold Medalist) and Paula Radcliffe (Marathon World Record Holder) were added to the database. The world-class athlete results had the same relationship as seen with the regular athletes.

A few of the very slowest full-marathon finish times were much slower than predicted from the half-marathon time for those athletes. This may be due to some slower athletes having less adaptation to running full-marathons or due to poor pacing. It is a big step-up from half-marathon to full marathon and many slower athletes run to a 'just-finish' strategy rather than attempting a fast result.

The chart on this page displays Marathon Finish Time in minutes (on the vertical y-axis) plotted against Half-Marathon Finish Time in minutes (on the horizontal x-axis). Each circle plotted on the chart indicates the pair of race results for each individual athlete. The fastest athlete is Mo Farah, who's circle is plotted on the bottom left of the chart.

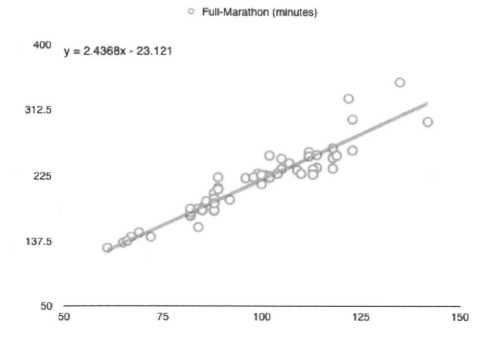

Based on this data, it is possible to predict how an individual will perform at the Marathon distance if we know that athlete's current Half-Marathon finish time. The first Table at the end of this chapter has been calculated using the formula derived from the chart above. The formula is $y = 2.4368x - 23.121$.

Iron-Run

Please note that for iron-distance triathlon, the target Marathon Finish Time should be about 30 minutes slower than for a standalone marathon.

Chose your Marathon Raceday Plan accordingly. This will be your fastest possible iron-distance run that could be achieved if the swim and cycle pacing was correct.

Do not be too disappointed if you do not always achieve this, because there are many things that may not go perfectly during an iron-distance race day.

Calculation of Your Personal Target Marathon Pace and Target Marathon Finish Time

This is clearly an imperfect science, because athletes can be inconsistent with their performances for many reasons including race conditions.

However, the predictive value of the tables on the next two pages is still useful in order to attempt perfect pacing for Marathon racing.

Firstly, estimate your Target Marathon Finish Time from the first Table, by using your previously achieved Half-Marathon Finish Time.

This should be your Half-Marathon Finish Time that relates to a time when you were at a similar level of fitness to now.

Secondly, use the second Table to estimate the Target Average Marathon Running Pace that will be required to achieve your Target Marathon Finish Time.

You need to know your Target Average Marathon Running Pace in order to create your mile-by-mile Marathon Race-Day Schedule. This is explained in chapter 21.

Dr Jim's Chart Predicting Marathon Finish Time from Half-Marathon

Half-M	Full-M	Half-M	Full-M	Half-M	Full-M	Half-M	Full-M
1:00	2:04	1:26	3:07	1:52	4:10	2:18	5:13
1:01	2:06	1:27	3:09	1:53	4:13	2:19	5:16
1:02	2:08	1:28	3:12	1:54	4:15	2:20	5:19
1:03	2:11	1:29	3:14	1:55	4:18	2:21	5:21
1:04	2:13	1:30	3:17	1:56	4:20	2:22	5:24
1:05	2:16	1:31	3:19	1:57	4:23	2:23	5:26
1:06	2:18	1:32	3:22	1:58	4:25	2:24	5:29
1:07	2:21	1:33	3:24	1:59	4:27	2:25	5:31
1:08	2:23	1:34	3:26	2:00	4:30	2:26	5:33
1:09	2:25	1:35	3:29	2:01	4:32	2:27	5:36
1:10	2:28	1:36	3:31	2:02	4:35	2:28	5:38
1:11	2:30	1:37	3:34	2:03	4:37	2:29	5:41
1:12	2:33	1:38	3:36	2:04	4:40	2:30	5:43
1:13	2:35	1:39	3:39	2:05	4:42	2:31	5:45
1:14	2:38	1:40	3:41	2:06	4:45	2:32	5:48
1:15	2:40	1:41	3:44	2:07	4:47	2:33	5:50
1:16	2:43	1:42	3:46	2:08	4:49	2:34	5:53
1:17	2:45	1:43	3:48	2:09	4:52	2:35	5:55
1:18	2:47	1:44	3:51	2:10	4:54	2:36	5:58
1:19	2:50	1:45	3:53	2:11	4:57	2:37	6:00
1:20	2:52	1:46	3:56	2:12	4:59	2:38	6:03
1:21	2:55	1:47	3:58	2:13	5:02	2:39	6:05
1:22	2:57	1:48	4:01	2:14	5:04	2:40	6:07
1:23	3:00	1:49	4:03	2:15	5:07	2:41	6:10
1:24	3:02	1:50	4:05	2:16	5:09	2:42	6:12
1:25	3:05	1:51	4:08	2:17	5:11	2:43	6:15

Dr Jim's Marathon Average Race Pace Calculator

Full-Marathon Finish Time	Average Pace (minutes: seconds per mile)	Full-Marathon Finish Time	Average Pace (minutes: seconds per mile)	Full-Marathon Finish Time	Average Pace (minutes: seconds per mile)	Full-Marathon Finish Time	Average Pace (minutes: seconds per mile)
2:04	4:43	3:07	7:08	4:10	9:32	5:13	11:56
2:06	4:48	3:09	7:12	4:13	9:39	5:16	12:03
2:08	4:53	3:12	7:19	4:15	9:43	5:19	12:10
2:11	4:59	3:14	7:24	4:18	9:50	5:21	12:14
2:13	5:04	3:17	7:31	4:20	9:55	5:24	12:21
2:16	5:11	3:19	7:35	4:23	10:02	5:26	12:26
2:18	5:15	3:22	7:42	4:25	10:06	5:29	12:33
2:21	5:22	3:24	7:47	4:27	10:11	5:31	12:38
2:23	5:27	3:26	7:51	4:30	10:18	5:33	12:42
2:25	5:31	3:29	7:58	4:32	10:22	5:36	12:49
2:28	5:38	3:31	8:03	4:35	10:29	5:38	12:54
2:30	5:43	3:34	8:09	4:37	10:34	5:41	13:00
2:33	5:50	3:36	8:14	4:40	10:41	5:43	13:05
2:35	5:54	3:39	8:21	4:42	10:45	5:45	13:10
2:38	6:01	3:41	8:25	4:45	10:52	5:48	13:16
2:40	6:06	3:44	8:32	4:47	10:57	5:50	13:21
2:43	6:13	3:46	8:37	4:49	11:01	5:53	13:28
2:45	6:17	3:48	8:41	4:52	11:08	5:55	13:32
2:47	6:22	3:51	8:48	4:54	11:13	5:58	13:39
2:50	6:29	3:53	8:53	4:57	11:20	6:00	13:44
2:52	6:33	3:56	9:00	4:59	11:24	6:03	13:51
2:55	6:40	3:58	9:04	5:02	11:31	6:05	13:55
2:57	6:45	4:01	9:11	5:04	11:36	6:07	14:00
3:00	6:52	4:03	9:16	5:07	11:42	6:10	14:07
3:02	6:56	4:05	9:20	5:09	11:47	6:12	14:11
3:05	7:03	4:08	9:27	5:11	11:52	6:15	14:18

CHAPTER 20

Marathon Race Strategy

Your fastest marathons will not be run with a constant Pace (minutes:seconds per mile) or a constant Heart Rate (HR). This is because you want to use every last ounce of available energy and be totally drained by the finish line.

Be prepared to run 26.5 miles rather than 26.2 miles, because you can rarely adhere precisely to the the shortest route. Other runners are likely to occupy the 'racing-line' in front of you when the course turns corners, so you may need to run around them in order to maintain your optimum pace.

During these 26.5 miles you will be employing a mixture of the aerobic and anaerobic systems in your body to turn fuel into power. If you did the whole marathon using the aerobic system alone, it would not be at your potential fastest average pace.

Fast marathon running is not to do with staying the whole time in your comfort zone. It requires you to hold-back initially, then gradually increase the effort level until towards the end you are making a massive frantic effort.

A perfectly paced marathon is 'a beautiful thing' and a wonderful experience. It will not happen in every race.

The optimum metabolic strategy is to run the first couple of miles exclusively using the almost unlimited supply of the aerobic system. Miles 1 and 2 warm-up the body fully without dipping into your limited anaerobic supplies.

In miles 3 to 6 you, are getting close to top speed for this race but hopefully without using very much of the anaerobic system. You will feel fantastic and mental discipline will be needed to hold-back a little. There is a very long way left to run and anaerobic energy reserves need be conserved.

During miles 7 to 10, you are at maximum speed for this marathon and it feels comfortable. Reflect on all the time and effort you invested in the training to get you to this situation. Smile, relax and enjoy it. Take care not to run faster than planned.

From mile 11 to 15, you need to raise your HR slightly in order to maintain pace. This is a sign of fatigue setting-in and a sign that the waste products of the anaerobic system are starting to reduce your efficiency.

Miles 16 to 20 can be tough, because your effort level (and therefore your HR) rises further in order to maintain speed. You must be mentally strong at this time, because there is still a long way to go.

At mile 21, you get the mental boost of knowing that the final phase has begun plus you feel better about yourself as you overtake other runners who are fading due to poor pacing. From mile 21 onwards you will need to raise the effort level and ensure that the HR does steadily rise.

In miles 22 and 23, you can start taking risks with your energy reserves and push yourself steadily harder. It will pay dividends in terms of speed without much chance of 'burning out', because the end is not far away now.

At mile 24, you know 'you've got this'. Smile. Very little can go wrong now. Keep going and prepare yourself for a big effort in mile 25.

By mile 25, you have very little energy reserve left but you are running on pride and happiness that the race has gone well. Your body is loaded with waste products of the anaerobic system so there needs to be a massive effort to maintain speed. You are going to make this penultimate mile into your final effort to get a fast finish time. You know that 'mile 26 will take care of itself'.

Mile 26 is the home stretch. You disengage your logical human brain and dip into the primate psyche of your ancestors. You find hidden reserves of energy and effort that are normally unavailable to you.

The crowd are shouting and you might be screaming yourself. A short time ago you thought you had nothing left in you, but now you make a super-human effort and run fast despite 'an empty tank'.

The last few hundred yards to the finish is a sprint. You might better your finish time by another 30 seconds in this last mad dash for the line.

You want to use up everything and take nothing home. Leave it all out there on the course. Do not let anybody overtake you.

<u>Do please ask permission from your physician (doctor) before attempting to raise your effort level (and heart rate) this high.</u>
<u>If you have health issues then you must stay within your comfort zone during the last few miles and not raise your effort level as described above.</u>

Negative Splits

This phrase means that the second half of the race was run quicker than the first half. Generally, this is desirable and a sign that pacing was good.

My current personal best (PB) of 2:51 was done with a 3 minute negative split (1:27 and 1:24). Such a large negative split suggests that the first half was too slow and I hope that maybe one day I can run 1:25 and 1:24.

Fuel and Fluids

Have a clear simple plan worked out in advance and practice this in training.

1. Do not get dehydrated or run out of fuel, as this damages your metabolic efficiency and inevitably hurts your finish time. Prevention is better than treatment here.

2. Consume little and often right from the start. Have a gel and a tiny drink in the starting pen. If you are doing an iron-distance triathlon, ensure that you hydrate and fuel-up correctly during the cycle to be in optimal condition to start the run.

3. If it is a hot day then have small drinks from mile 2 onwards. On a normal day you can delay this until

mile 3 or 4 in order to reduce the risk of early over-hydrating and then needing a toilet stop.

4. From mile 4 onwards, make sure you drink at every mile (and carry a small drink bottle if the race does not have drink stations at every mile).

With a fast-paced marathon you will inevitably be a bit dehydrated by the finish and **absorbing too much** fluid is almost impossible. Conversely, **drinking too much** during the race can occur and cause a bloated stomach, so there is a sensible balance to be struck.

Practice your drinking strategy in training and in Grade B races (well ahead of your target Grade A Marathon race).

5. Too much salt intake is better than too little, so carry salt with you to take during the race. Approximately one salt tablet for each hour of running is recommended, but race conditions and different sweat rates between individuals mean you may need to vary this.

6. Even though your training has made you more efficient at fat-burning, you still need glucose from energy gels during a fast-paced marathon. Avoid 'hitting the wall' by consuming a gel every 2 to 3 miles (from mile 4 onwards). It may be best to consume half a gel then hold the rest in your hand in order to consume the rest a few minutes or a mile later (this may help digestion).

CHAPTER 21

Marathon Race-Day Plans

Here are detailed (mile-by-mile) marathon race plans for ages from 18 years to 75 years and for Finish Times from 2:14 to 6:29. These are also called marathon race schedules. Plan is synonymous with schedule in this context.

As discussed elsewhere in this book, runners should chose the precise details of their race schedule according to their own personal maximum heart rate (HRmax). Age is no more than an approximation for HRmax in this context.

If you plan to run your marathon for reasons other than getting your fastest possible time, enjoy it and don't stress too much about your heart rate and pace. Nevertheless, always start the marathon gently then get to the target pace by around mile 4. Avoid sharp increases in pace at any time apart from the last few hundred yards (as you dash for the finish line).

Do please ask permission from your physician (doctor) before attempting to raise your heart rate high. If in doubt, you must stay within your comfort zone and not raise your effort level during the last few miles of the Marathon race.

The Marathon race plan (Tables 1A and 1B) is an example that is specifically for a runner with maximum Heart Rate (HRmax) of 180 bpm (which is typical for a 40 year old) who has a target Marathon Finish Time of 2:59.

Runners with different HRmax and different target Marathon Finish Time should use Tables 2 to 6 (found further on in this chapter) in order to get the HR's and running pace required for their own specific needs. The mile by mile strategy and advice in the Marathon race plan is the same for everyone.

Table 1A. Marathon Race Plan for 2:59 Finish Time and HRmax 180

Mile number	Heart Rate	Min:Sec per mile	Strategy	Comments and Advice
		6:49 average pace		
1	HRmax-40 = 140	7:30	Stay aerobic and don't let HR spike	Don't chase after faster runners
2	HRmax-35 = 145	7:00	Edging towards average race pace	Relax as there is a long way left to go
3	HRmax-33 = 147	6:50	Fully warmed up	start drinking
4	HRmax-30 = 150	6:48	drink every mile	gel every 2-3 miles
5	HRmax-30 = 150	6:48	smile	
6	HRmax-30 = 150	6:48		good running form
7	HRmax-28 = 152	6:46	be positive	
8	HRmax-28 = 152	6:46		enjoy the scenery
9	HRmax-28 = 152	6:46	feeling comfortable	
10	HRmax-28 = 152	6:46		
11	HRmax-25 = 150	6:46	raise HR a little to maintain pace	slight fatigue starting to set in
12	HRmax-25 = 150	6:46		
13	HRmax-25 = 150	6:46	keep steady pace and HR	crowds cheer at half-way but stay calm

Table 1B. Marathon Race Plan for 2:59 Finish Time and HRmax 180

Mile number	Heart Rate	Min:Sec per mile	Strategy	Comments and Advice
		6:49 average pace		
14	HRmax-25 = 150	6:46	1:30 on the clock	Half the race done
15	HRmax-25 = 150	6:46	Keep this steady pace until mile 20	Don't get excited
16	HRmax-20 = 155	6:46		
17	HRmax-20 = 155	6:46		
18	HRmax-20 = 155	6:46		
19	HRmax-20 = 155	6:46	2 more miles at this effort level then final phase begins	As the race goes longer you get stronger
20	HRmax-20 = 155	6:48	Will be great to finish mile 20 and not "hit the wall"	You may slow slightly but you overtake people
21	HRmax-18 = 157	6:48	It's ok to raise HR a little to maintain pace	Much good work done now so you must finish the job
22	HRmax-18 = 157	6:48	Into the last 5 miles	Don't let anybody overtake you now
23	HRmax-18 = 157	6:48	Do not slow down	Smile
24	HRmax-18 = 157	6:50	Raise effort a little and take some risks with your energy reserves	The end is near. You've got this!
25	HRmax-15 = 160	6:50	Make this a fast mile	The mile after this one will take care of itself
26	HRmax-10 = 165	6:50	The cheers of the crowd will get you home now	Use up any energy you have left and do not slow down
0.2 to 0.5	HRmax-5 = 170	6:30	Sprint like your life depended on it	Good job!

209

Tables 2, 3 and 4 show the pace required for each mile for other target Marathon Finish Times from 2:14 to 6:14.

Table 2. Dr Jim's Marathon Race Schedule for Finish Times between 2:14 to 3:29

Mile Number, Heart Rate (HR)	5:06 average Pace for a 2:14 finish (min:sec / mile)	5:41 average Pace for a 2:29 finish (min:sec / mile)	6:15 average Pace for a 2:44 finish (min:sec / mile)	6:49 average Pace for a 2:59 finish (min:sec / mile)	7:24 average Pace for a 3:14 finish (min:sec / mile)	7:58 average Pace for a 3:29 finish (min:sec / mile)
mile 1, HRmax-40	5:50	6:25	7:00	7:30	8:00	8:30
mile 2, HRmax-35	5:15	5:50	6:25	7:00	7:30	8:00
mile 3, HRmax-33	5:08	5:43	6:18	6:50	7:25	8:00
mile 4, HRmax-30	5:05	5:40	6:14	6:48	7:23	7:57
mile 5, HRmax-30	5:05	5:40	6:14	6:48	7:23	7:57
mile 6, HRmax-30	5:05	5:40	6:14	6:48	7:23	7:57
mile 7, HRmax-28	5:03	5:38	6:12	6:46	7:21	7:55
mile 8, HRmax-28	5:03	5:38	6:12	6:46	7:21	7:55
mile 9, HRmax-28	5:03	5:38	6:12	6:46	7:21	7:55
mile 10, HRmax-28	5:03	5:38	6:12	6:46	7:21	7:55
mile 11, HRmax-25	5:03	5:38	6:12	6:46	7:21	7:55
mile 12, HRmax-25	5:03	5:38	6:12	6:46	7:21	7:55
mile 13, HRmax-25	5:03	5:38	6:12	6:46	7:21	7:55
mile 14, HRmax-25	5:03	5:38	6:12	6:46	7:21	7:55
mile 15, HRmax-25	5:03	5:38	6:12	6:46	7:21	7:55
mile 16, HRmax-20	5:03	5:38	6:12	6:46	7:21	7:55
mile 17, HRmax-20	5:03	5:38	6:12	6:46	7:21	7:55
mile 18, HRmax-20	5:03	5:38	6:12	6:46	7:21	7:55
mile 19, HRmax-20	5:03	5:38	6:12	6:46	7:21	7:55
mile 20, HRmax-20	5:05	5:40	6:14	6:48	7:23	7:57
mile 21, HRmax-18	5:05	5:40	6:14	6:48	7:23	7:57
mile 22, HRmax-18	5:05	5:40	6:14	6:48	7:23	7:57
mile 23, HRmax-18	5:05	5:40	6:14	6:48	7:23	7:57
mile 24, HRmax-18	5:08	5:43	6:18	6:50	7:25	8:00
mile 25, HRmax-15	5:08	5:43	6:18	6:50	7:25	8:00
mile 26, HRmax-10	5:08	5:43	6:18	6:50	7:25	8:00
last 0.2 to 0.5 miles, HRmax-5	5:00	5:30	6:00	6:30	7:00	7:30

211

Table 3. Dr Jim's Marathon Race Schedule for Finish Times between 3:44 and 4:59

Mile Number, Heart Rate (HR)	8:32 average Pace for a **3:44** finish (min:sec / mile)	9:07 average Pace for a **3:59** finish (min:sec / mile)	9:41 average Pace for a **4:14** finish (min:sec / mile)	10:16 average Pace for a **4:29** finish (min:sec / mile)	10:50 average Pace for a **4:44** finish (min:sec / mile)	11:24 average Pace for a **4:59** finish (min:sec / mile)
mile 1, HRmax-40	9:00	9:35	10:10	10:45	11:20	11:55
mile 2, HRmax-35	8:35	9:10	9:44	10:19	10:53	11:27
mile 3, HRmax-33	8:35	9:10	9:44	10:19	10:53	11:27
mile 4, HRmax-30	8:32	9:07	9:42	10:17	10:50	11:24
mile 5, HRmax-30	8:32	9:07	9:42	10:17	10:50	11:24
mile 6, HRmax-30	8:32	9:07	9:42	10:17	10:50	11:24
mile 7, HRmax-28	8:30	9:05	9:39	10:14	10:48	11:22
mile 8, HRmax-28	8:30	9:05	9:39	10:14	10:48	11:22
mile 9, HRmax-28	8:30	9:05	9:39	10:14	10:48	11:22
mile 10, HRmax-28	8:30	9:05	9:39	10:14	10:48	11:22
mile 11, HRmax-25	8:30	9:05	9:39	10:14	10:48	11:22
mile 12, HRmax-25	8:30	9:05	9:39	10:14	10:48	11:22
mile 13, HRmax-25	8:30	9:05	9:39	10:14	10:48	11:22
mile 14, HRmax-25	8:30	9:05	9:39	10:14	10:48	11:22
mile 15, HRmax-25	8:30	9:05	9:39	10:14	10:48	11:22
mile 16, HRmax-20	8:30	9:05	9:39	10:14	10:48	11:22
mile 17, HRmax-20	8:30	9:05	9:39	10:14	10:48	11:22
mile 18, HRmax-20	8:30	9:05	9:39	10:14	10:48	11:22
mile 19, HRmax-20	8:30	9:05	9:39	10:14	10:48	11:22
mile 20, HRmax-20	8:32	9:07	9:42	10:17	10:48	11:22
mile 21, HRmax-18	8:32	9:07	9:42	10:17	10:48	11:22
mile 22, HRmax-18	8:32	9:07	9:42	10:17	10:48	11:22
mile 23, HRmax-18	8:32	9:07	9:42	10:17	10:48	11:22
mile 24, HRmax-18	8:34	9:10	9:44	10:19	10:53	11:27
mile 25, HRmax-15	8:34	9:10	9:44	10:19	10:53	11:27
mile 26, HRmax-10	8:34	9:10	9:44	10:19	10:53	11:27
last 0.2 to 0.5 miles, HRmax-5	8:00	8:30	9:00	9:30	10:00	10:30

Table 4. Dr Jim's Marathon Race Schedule for Finish Times between 5:14 and 6:29

Mile Number, Heart Rate (HR)	11:59 average Pace for a 5:14 finish (min:sec / mile)	12:33 average Pace for a 5:29 finish (min:sec / mile)	13:07 average Pace for a 5:44 finish (min:sec / mile)	13:42 average Pace for a 5:59 finish (min:sec / mile)	14:16 average Pace for a 6:14 finish (min:sec / mile)	14:50 average Pace for a 6:29 finish (min:sec / mile)
mile 1, HRmax-40	12:10	12:45	13:20	13:55	14:30	15:05
mile 2, HRmax-35	12:05	12:35	13:10	13:45	14:18	14:52
mile 3, HRmax-33	12:05	12:35	13:10	13:45	14:18	14:52
mile 4, HRmax-30	12:00	12:35	13:10	13:45	14:18	14:52
mile 5, HRmax-30	12:00	12:35	13:10	13:45	14:18	14:52
mile 6, HRmax-30	12:00	12:35	13:10	13:45	14:18	14:52
mile 7, HRmax-28	11:57	12:31	13:05	13:40	14:18	14:52
mile 8, HRmax-28	11:57	12:31	13:05	13:40	14:14	14:48
mile 9, HRmax-28	11:57	12:31	13:05	13:40	14:14	14:48
mile 10, HRmax-28	11:57	12:31	13:05	13:40	14:14	14:48
mile 11, HRmax-25	11:57	12:31	13:05	13:40	14:14	14:48
mile 12, HRmax-25	11:57	12:31	13:05	13:40	14:14	14:48
mile 13, HRmax-25	11:57	12:31	13:05	13:40	14:14	14:48
mile 14, HRmax-25	11:57	12:31	13:05	13:40	14:14	14:48
mile 15, HRmax-25	11:57	12:31	13:05	13:40	14:14	14:48
mile 16, HRmax-20	11:57	12:31	13:05	13:40	14:14	14:48
mile 17, HRmax-20	11:57	12:31	13:05	13:40	14:14	14:48
mile 18, HRmax-20	11:57	12:31	13:05	13:40	14:14	14:48
mile 19, HRmax-20	11:57	12:31	13:05	13:40	14:14	14:48
mile 20, HRmax-20	11:57	12:31	13:05	13:40	14:14	14:48
mile 21, HRmax-18	11:57	12:31	13:05	13:40	14:18	14:52
mile 22, HRmax-18	11:57	12:35	13:10	13:45	14:18	14:52
mile 23, HRmax-18	11:57	12:35	13:10	13:45	14:18	14:52
mile 24, HRmax-18	12:05	12:35	13:10	13:45	14:18	14:52
mile 25, HRmax-15	12:05	12:35	13:10	13:45	14:18	14:52
mile 26, HRmax-10	12:05	12:35	13:10	13:45	14:18	14:52
last 0.2 to 0.5 miles, HRmax-5	11:00	11:30	12:00	12:30	13:00	13:30

213

Tables 5 and 6 show Heart Rate (HR) for each mile for different HRmax from 200 - 145 (which are typical for athletes aged between 18 and 75).

Table 5. HR's for Marathon Race (HRmax 200 to 175 bpm)

	HR for each mile HRmax = 200 bpm	HR for each mile HRmax = 195 bpm	HR for each mile HRmax = 190 bpm	HR for each mile HRmax = 185 bpm	HR for each mile HRmax = 180 bpm	HR for each mile HRmax = 175 bpm
	average age 18-20	average for age 25	average for age 30	average for age 35	average for age 40	average for age 45
HRmax-40, mile 1	160	155	150	145	140	135
HRmax-35, mile 2	165	160	155	150	145	140
HRmax-33, mile 3	167	162	157	152	147	142
HRmax-30, mile 4	170	165	160	155	150	145
HRmax-30, mile 5	170	165	160	155	150	145
HRmax-30, mile 6	170	165	160	155	150	145
HRmax-28, mile 7	172	167	162	157	152	147
HRmax-28, mile 8	172	167	162	157	152	147
HRmax-28, mile 9	172	167	162	157	152	147
HRmax-28, mile 10	172	167	162	157	152	147
HRmax-25, mile 11	175	170	165	160	155	150
HRmax-25, mile 12	175	170	165	160	155	150
HRmax-25, mile 13	175	170	165	160	155	150
HRmax-25, mile 14	175	170	165	160	155	150
HRmax-25, mile 15	175	170	165	160	155	150
HRmax-20, mile 16	180	175	170	165	160	155
HRmax-20, mile 17	180	175	170	165	160	155
HRmax-20, mile 18	180	175	170	165	160	155
HRmax-20, mile 19	180	175	170	165	160	155
HRmax-20, mile 20	180	175	170	165	160	155
HRmax-18, mile 21	182	177	172	167	162	157
HRmax-18, mile 22	182	177	172	167	162	157
HRmax-18, mile 23	182	177	172	167	162	157
HRmax-18, mile 24	182	177	172	167	162	157
HRmax-15, mile 25	185	180	175	170	165	160
HRmax-10, mile 26	190	185	180	175	170	165
HRmax-5, to finish	195	190	185	180	175	170

Table 6. HR's for Marathon Race (HRmax 170 to 145 bpm)

	HR for each mile HRmax = 170 bpm	HR for each mile HRmax = 165 bpm	HR for each mile HRmax = 160 bpm	HR for each mile HRmax = 155 bpm	HR for each mile HRmax = 150 bpm	HR for each mile HRmax = 145 bpm
	average for age 50	average for age 55	average for age 60	average for age 65	average for age 70	average for age 75
HRmax-40, mile 1	130	125	120	115	110	115
HRmax-35, mile 2	135	130	125	120	115	110
HRmax-33, mile 3	137	132	127	122	117	112
HRmax-30, mile 4	140	135	130	125	120	115
HRmax-30, mile 5	140	135	130	125	120	115
HRmax-30, mile 6	140	135	130	125	120	115
HRmax-28, mile 7	142	137	132	127	122	117
HRmax-28, mile 8	142	137	132	127	122	117
HRmax-28, mile 9	142	137	132	127	122	117
HRmax-28, mile 10	142	137	132	127	122	117
HRmax-25, mile 11	145	140	135	130	125	120
HRmax-25, mile 12	145	140	135	130	125	120
HRmax-25, mile 13	145	140	135	130	125	120
HRmax-25, mile 14	145	140	135	130	125	120
HRmax-25, mile 15	145	140	135	130	125	120
HRmax-20, mile 16	150	145	140	135	130	125
HRmax-20, mile 17	150	145	140	135	130	125
HRmax-20, mile 18	150	145	140	135	130	125
HRmax-20, mile 19	150	145	140	135	130	125
HRmax-20, mile 20	150	145	140	135	130	125
HRmax-18, mile 21	152	147	142	137	132	127
HRmax-18, mile 22	152	147	142	137	132	127
HRmax-18, mile 23	152	147	142	137	132	127
HRmax-18, mile 24	152	147	142	137	132	127
HRmax-15, mile 25	155	150	145	140	135	130
HRmax-10, mile 26	160	155	150	145	140	135
HRmax-5, to finish	165	160	155	150	145	140

For iron-distance triathlon, the target Marathon Finish Time should be about 30 minutes slower than for a standalone marathon and your HR will be around 10 bpm slower at every stage. Chose your Marathon Raceday Plan accordingly.

This will be your fastest possible iron-distance run that could be achieved if the swim and cycle pacing was correct.

Section D

"Finish"

CHAPTER 22

Illegal Performance Enhancement

Drug cheats get side effects. Don't do it !

It is worth looking at the WADA web-site to get some understanding of the variety of illegal substances and some of the complexities involved.

Personally, I don't see that any of these substances would make me run a faster marathon. There is no justification to break rules, attempt to cheat or expose oneself to potentially harmful substances.

I do understand that there are some possible dilemmas and potential misunderstandings that could make somebody make a mistake.

Some of the banned substances do have perfectly legitimate medical uses and many people do need to take them (for instance asthma inhalers and steroid creams).

WADA list

https://www.wada-ama.org/en/what-we-do/prohibited-list
Since 2004, and as mandated by World Anti-Doping Code, WADA has published an annual List of Prohibited Substances and Methods (List).
The List, which forms one of the five International Standards, identifies the substances and methods prohibited in- and out-of-competition, and in particular sports.

The substances and methods on the list are classified by different categories. These categories include steroids, erythropoietin and stimulants.

Examples of abused substances include:

1. Anabolic Steroids

These promote muscle growth. Marathon runners do not need big muscles and indeed big muscles would slow down endurance runners. Do not take anabolic steroids.

2. Epo (Erythropoietin-Receptor agonists) and Blood Transfusion

These methods increase the oxygen carrying capacity of the body by increasing the blood concentration of red-blood cells and haemoglobin.

This is blatant cheating and is also dangerous. The increased viscosity of the blood caused by these methods raises the risks of blocked blood vessels. Blocked blood vessels cause things such as stroke and heart attack. Neither Epo nor Transfusions should ever be used to try to improve athletic performance.

The benefit of having increased blood oxygen carrying capacity is difficult to quantify for marathon running but it may be only a small benefit.

The same effect can be achieved safely and perfectly legally by doing altitude training (see next section of this book).

3. Stimulants

Marathon racing is more to do with conserving energy and not getting too excited.

Coffee (caffeine) is legal and provides more than enough stimulant effect for the final part of the marathon when you may need a boost.

Caffeinated gels are useful to carry with you for the race and indeed these are often available at race feed stations.

You must avoid coffee/caffeine if you know it has harmful effects on you or your physician (doctor) does not advise you to have caffeine.

Illegal stimulants include cocaine and amphetamines. Please do not take any of these dangerous illegal substances.

CHAPTER 23

Legal Performance Enhancement

Coffee/Caffeine

Caffeine is part of most people's everyday nutrition and it is perfectly legal for use in sports such as Marathon Running and Triathlon.

You must avoid coffee/caffeine if you know it has harmful effects on you or your physician (doctor) does not advise you to have caffeine.

Caffeine has important performance enhancing effects and most athletes will either use it routinely or use it sometimes.

1. Raises arousal level (including raised heart rate).
2. Reduces the perceived level of effort.
3. Keeps you awake.
4. Some energy gel/drink manufacturers claim that caffeine increases the rate of glucose absorption from the stomach.

Taurine

There are several drinks (e.g. Red Bull) that contain Caffeine and also Taurine.

Taurine is a naturally occurring amino-acid (protein building block) that is present in a wide range of the body tissue of animals and humans. Taurine makes up around 0.1% of human body weight.

It is legal to consume Taurine, but I tend to avoid it and I doubt it is significantly helpful to many marathon runners. Though taurine is naturally occurring it cannot be said to be totally without unwanted effects (like most things encountered in life).

Altitude Training (AT)

This is a perfectly legal and effective way to increase the oxygen carrying capacity of the blood. Most professional athletes will have tried this at some time but it is impractical for most amateurs to do.

The best way to do AT is to 'Sleep High and Train Low'. Sleep at high altitude then descend much nearer to sea level to do the day's training before returning to high altitude for rest and sleep.

The oxygen concentration in air at high altitude is significantly lower than at low altitude. We all know that it is harder to breath at the top of a mountain because 'the air is thinner'.

Spending the majority of each 24 hour period at high altitude, stimulates the body to adapt by raising the amount of the oxygen-carrying molecule in the blood. This oxygen-carrying molecule is called

Haemoglobin (Hb) and it is red in colour when bound to oxygen.

Some training can be done at high altitude, but the 'thin air' severely limits the ability to do high intensity exercise. Therefore, it is ideal to descend to lower altitude for daytime training.

Most people do not have access to a location where they can sleep at high altitude. However, one can legally create high altitude conditions in an Altitude Tent. Buy or rent an Altitude Simulator machine with an air-tight tent to go with it for sleeping in.

I have never done this myself and I do not know anybody who has done it. There is clearly a market for AT equipment for athletes and for mountaineers, because there are numerous companies to be found on the internet trading with this product.

It takes a couple of weeks of AT for the body to make meaningful adaptations and these adaptations will be lost within a couple of weeks away from altitude.

It is not clear exactly how much marathon performance enhancement can be gained with AT, but even a tiny benefit could mean the difference between finishing first or fourth at the Olympic Games.

The altitude required to make a significant effect is generally believed to be above 2,100 metres (6,900 feet). Above 2,400 metres (8,000 feet) is thought to be ideal.

Here are some popular locations:
Mammoth Lakes, California (2,400m)
Iten, Kenya (2,400m)
Dullstroom, South Africa (2,100m)
Sierra Nevada, Spain (2,300m)

Most amateur athletes do not consider that the effort and inconvenience of AT is worthwhile. However, they might consider taking a vacation in a mountain resort shortly before a big race.

Heat Acclimatisation (HA)

If you live and train in a cold climate but intend to race somewhere hot, then HA is worth doing.

You may need to do HA if you take a trip to run a marathon in a different hemisphere. The seasons will be different, so it is best to prepare properly.

The adaptations required for optimal racing in the heat take around 10 to 14 days to develop. Gradual adaptation is required, as with every other thing we do in training, so start HA a couple of weeks before arriving at the race venue.

Changes that our bodies make in response to HA are related to sweat rate and perceived fatigue amongst other things, but there is no need to know all the details as it all happens automatically when we prepare properly.

Please be cautious with exercise in the heat or when wearing extra layers, because excessive overheating is dangerous and this can easily occur.

However, I have successfully done HA on a number of occasions, including preparing for the tropic heat and humidity in Hawaii. Here is how:

1. Wear extra layers of clothing at all times (including in bed).

2. Train with extra layers (including hat and gloves).

3. Wear HR monitor to provide warning signs that you are overheating.

4. Do HA training sessions for shorter duration or lower intensity than normal in order to avoid severe overheating or dehydration.

5. Take off layers of clothing immediately if you do overheat.

6. Heat-stress or heat-stroke is dangerous and does damage the body (and the brain) so if you overheat it may harm athletic performance for weeks afterwards.

7. A thermometer is the best way to be alerted to overheating. I have never run wearing a thermometer but presumably it would not be impossible to do so.

8. During HA you should drink more than twice as much isotonic drink (or water with salt) as you would normally drink whilst running.

9. Arrive at race venue several days (ideally more than a week) before the race in order to do some running in conditions as they will be on race day.

LCHF Diet (Low Carb Healthy Fat or Low Carb High Fat)

I have found LCHF to be highly effective at improving marathon performance and there are further details in the nutrition section.

LCHF diet makes the body more adapted to using fat as fuel, thereby increasing the aerobic system's contribution to power production. The body then requires a smaller amount of power production using the anaerobic system.

It is the exhaustion of the anaerobic system's reserves plus the accumulation of waste products from the anaerobic system which are the main causes of fatigue during a marathon.

Adaptations resulting from the LCHF diet allow marathon runners to run faster for longer and with reduced chance of 'hitting the wall'.

Information about LCHF food can be found in the Nutrition Section in chapter 5 and the Recipes Section in chapter 17.

CHAPTER 24

Dr Jim's Journey

First marathon finish of 4:46 in 2008. This achievement was quite decent for a 45-year old with no significant sporting background who was working hard as a busy physician as well as being a husband and father of three children.

What occurred after that has been (and continues to be) a wonderful journey of discovery and self-improvement.

Marathon running and triathlon steadily became a passion that relieved stress, improved health and triggered many friendships.

The facts speak for themselves when considering the methods used. Fitter and faster now at age 53 than ever before. Marathon times steadily reduced so that by 2014 the personal best (PB) was 2:52 and by 2016 it is now 2:51.

Pleasingly, my Ironman Triathlon PB has steadily improved from 13:12 in 2009 to 9:45 in 2015.

There has also been the unexpected result of finishing in the top half of the 50-54 age group at the 2016 Ironman World Championship in Kona, Hawaii.

	standalone marathon 26.2 mile	Ironman run 26.2 mile
2008	4:46 at Hastings Marathon	no IM (Ironman Triathlon)
2009	4:30 at IM Bolton	4:30 at IM Bolton (13:12 overall)
2010	3:29 at Brighton Marathon	4:06 at IM Bolton
2011	3:11 at Abingdon Marathon	no IM
2012	3:01 at Abingdon Marathon	3:54 at IM Lanzarote
2013	2:56 at London Marathon	3:44 at IM Bolton
2014	2:52 at Brighton Marathon	3:26 at IM Florida
2015	2:59 at London Marathon	3:32 at IM Barcelona (9:45 overall)
2016	2:51 at Brighton Marathon	3:53 at IM Kona

Triathlon is a superb sport in its own right and it really compliments Marathon training, as has been explained already in this book.

Having studied the available information on this subject and learned from many inspirational people, there is plenty of knowledge that I want to pass on.

Many of my medical colleagues and patients have kindly listened to what I have to say on this subject and gratifyingly many of them have benefited from following these tips.

I am an ordinary middle-aged guy (in athletic terms) with ordinary genes and a busy life, training in his spare time.

The methods in this book do also apply to those with disabilities or indeed those lucky enough to have inherited elite physiology.

Thank you for reading this book. I do hope that you find it helpful and I would love to get your feedback (and race results).

Despite many hours of writing and checking for errors, some mistakes may remain within the pages of this book (hopefully nothing significant).

Best Wishes. Dr Jim.

drjimauthor@btinternet.com

Spectators gathered near the beach for the sunrise swim start at the 2016 Ironman Triathlon World Championship in Kona, Hawaii.

The day finished with a 26.2 mile run.

CHAPTER 25

Acknowledgements

I would like to think that throughout this journey, my medical career and family commitments have not been neglected. However, I am extremely grateful for everyone's support and understanding.

My lovely wife, Helen, has totally embraced this sporting and lifestyle adventure. Often Helen has been far ahead of me, for instance with nutrition and new sporting challenges.

Helen used to say that she "had never been a sporty person" but subsequently Helen has transformed herself into an accomplished runner/triathlete who can run a 3:34 Marathon and has completed a 50 mile multi-terrain running race.

Helen has combined this with all her other roles as a mother, wife, physician, and carer for her father.

Mid Sussex Triathlon Club has been the 'bed-rock' of our running and social network. There are just over 100 active members and they are all a positive influence on our physical and psychological wellbeing.

Many of these club members are extremely inspiring. Some are honoured in this book and I regret not having enough book space for many more.

Presumably, there are a huge number of clubs like this all over the world. It is a terrific local and international community to be part of.

'Park run' organise free, weekly, 5km timed runs in a multitude of locations around the world. They are open to everyone. These runs are safe and easy to take part in. I am grateful to the organisers of these events. I have enjoyed running and volunteering with 'Park run'.

https://www.parkrun.org.uk

'Lucky Jim' is grateful for a great family, good health, great friends and good fortune. Some things seem beyond our control (though switching lockers to 249 is an option).

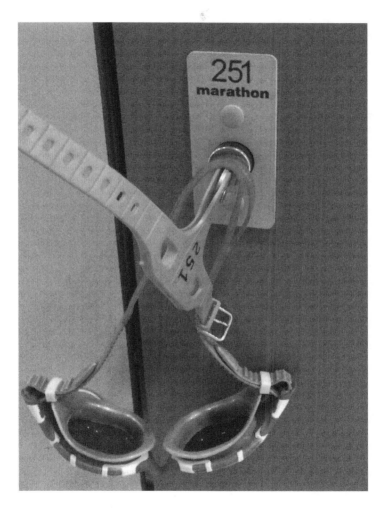

Swimming helped me run a 2:51 Marathon, which may have been fate because 251 is my locker number at the pool and 'marathon' is the locker brand.

Thanks Mum for (amongst many other things) teaching me to write and for suggesting this book title.

Thanks Dad for teaching me to be resilient, courageous, resolute, happy and modest (a work in progress).

Thanks to my brother Neil for being a great role model with a terrific sense of humour and superb cycling ability.

Book club friends (Hugo, Howard, Justin, Hefydd, John, Stephen and Martyn) have been instrumental in developing my interest in writing.

In 2008, Martyn was the first person I had ever met who had done a sub-3 hour marathon. He got me to enter my first marathon, then finished it almost 2 hours quicker than me.

Helen, Hefydd and Jeff provided photographs for this book as well as being generally supportive.

Johnny has been a great person to discuss the book concept with and he provided a peaceful retreat for me to do some writing.

Steve was the first person that I met who had competed at Kona and I have greatly valued his wise counsel.

Jean, David, Hugo and Monty did important proof-reading for me. However, I take full responsibility for any mistakes that remain.

Ant gave support and helpful advice on photography and publishing.

Trevor gave welcome feedback on book cover design.

Roger of the Mid Sussex Times has been a wonderful supporter of my humble efforts to raise money for the Alzheimer's Society with my racing and writing.

Friend and formidable racing rival, Mike, gave useful feedback on this book's training schedules.

Darren, Lucy and Ronak have been wonderful at discussing book ideas and commenting on the content in this publication.

CHAPTER 26

The Alzheimer's Society

The Alzheimer's Society is a charity that is dedicated to tackling one of the most important health challenges that we face.

The incidence of dementia is steadily rising and it is not confined to old age.

Many of us have friends and relatives with dementia.

This book is dedicated to my father-in law, who has become very disabled by dementia. Bill is a wonderful man .

At the time of writing this book, it is unclear what 'overheads' and publishing costs will be encountered. However, a portion of profits from sales will be donated to the Alzheimer's Society.

Thank you for purchasing this book.

https://www.alzheimers.org.uk

The word dementia describes a set of symptoms that may include memory loss and difficulties with thinking, problem-solving or language. Dementia is caused when the brain is damaged by diseases, such as Alzheimer's disease or a series of strokes. Dementia is progressive, which means the symptoms will gradually get worse.

There are many ways to help with the fight against dementia. From making a monthly donation, signing up to fundraising events, volunteering in your local area or getting involved in campaigning issues.

Section E

"Kona"

CHAPTER 27

Ironman World Championship

This is a supplementary section that was added to create a special edition of the book to celebrate the efforts of organisers, volunteers and participants in the Mid Sussex Triathlon Race held each June in Burgess Hill.

History of Ironman

Ironman first took place in 1978 with just 15 competitors. The concept was to create a massive endurance challenge that involved running the Honolulu Marathon Course in Hawaii, straight after a 2.4 mile ocean swim plus a 112 mile road cycle. At the time, nobody knew if this challenge would be completed by any of the competitors. Despite heat, humidity and rudimentary support facilities there were 12 finishers. Former Navy Seal, John Dunbar, lead for much of that first race but he became dehydrated and was overtaken with five miles of the marathon left to run. A Honolulu Cab Driver, Gordon Haller, won in 11:46 after running the last five miles in a remarkable 31 minutes.

In 1981, the race moved from Honolulu to the less urbanised location of Big Island, Hawaii. Start and finish are in the small seaside town of Kailua-Kona, which is often simply called Kona. The event has remained here ever since and it has become hugely popular. For many years now, race entry has been by qualification only. The competition for places in this race gets more intense each year.

Kona is the iconic Triathlon venue and you don't need to be racing in the main event in order to participate or enjoy the experience. Kona is a lovely super-friendly town with lots of preliminary events, banquets, tourism and partying. Being a volunteer marshal for the main race is really rewarding. The whole town is a giant expo for race week and there are loads of free items given out such as hats, shirts, gels, lubricants and cycle-bottles. There are numerous professional athletes and former world champions to spot, listen to and chat with.

WTC (World Triathlon Corporation) have this race week as their annual celebration. Everything is lavish and grand, despite there being a relatively small select group of main event racers compared to 'mega-races' like Roth or Frankfurt.

Dr Jim's Kona 2016 Race Report

Background

Inevitably, long distance triathlon would have arisen eventually in one or several places in the world. The fact that Hawaii was the location that established the specific iron race distances is probably fundamental to the current huge appeal of triathlon. This course and the professional athletes who have excelled here have become legendary.

Imagine being in a sauna for up to seventeen hours doing continual multi-sport. That is what the Ironman World Championship is like. However, Kailua-Kona in

Hawaii is a beautiful tropical paradise with very hospitable friendly locals, so the race is an absolute pleasure despite the challenging conditions.

It is a humbling experience. Many elite athletes in their prime, despite their Ironman podium finishes in other races, fail to finish at Kona or get beaten by senior citizen age-groupers.

Getting a slot

Currently about a quarter of a million athletes compete each year in qualifying races to try to get one of a couple of thousand places to the Ironman World Championship in Kailua-Kona, Big Island, Hawaii on the second Saturday each October. Some events seem a bit easier than others for qualifying but you always need to finish in the top 1-2% of age group.

Annually, there are about 100 legacy slots distributed amongst those who have completed more than a dozen official Ironman full-distance races. There are a handful of executive and charity places available in order to raise money for good causes. One charity is currently asking for a thirty-five thousand pound bond/pledge from the athlete who takes the single slot that they have for 2017.

There are a handful of slots for disabled athletes and for the US military.

There are about 100 professional slots, but obviously those are impossible for normal human beings to get. This year there were only 9 UK professionals good enough to reach this standard and 2 of these failed to finish.

Pre-race Training

Getting a Kona slot is a bit overwhelming, because of the thought of competing with the world's best. Even if you have your best race ever, you will still most likely rank low in age group and finish considerably slower than PB (personal best).

I decided to do a series of races to get me in shape and to bundle all this into a challenge to honour my father-in-law who has Alzheimer's disease. https://www.justgiving.com/fundraising/James-Graham19 Training was all about doing this series of races then avoiding injury in order to get to the Kona start-line intact.

3/4/16 Paris Marathon in 2:59
17/4/16 Brighton Marathon in 2:51 (PB)
24/4/16 London Marathon in 2:55
21/5/16 Lanzarote Ironman 140.7 in 13:56 (bike broke)
11/9/16 Weymouth Ironman 70.3 in 5:38
18/9/16 Wales ironman 140.7 in 11:27

Pre-race week

Kona exceeded all expectations. As soon as you get off the plane it is clear that Hawaiians take great pride in being kind, patient and hospitable. This is literally an island paradise and also the Ironman event does live up to the 'hype'.

My wife, Helen, probably had a better week than me because there was so much great stuff to do and no worries for her about saving energy for the big race.

- Ho'ala swim race 3.8km
- PATH 10km run race
- Underpants Run 1.5miles
- Traditional feasts x2
- Heroes of Hawaii banquet
- All World Athlete Breakfast with Dave Scott and Mark Allen
- Parade of Nations
- Welcome banquet
- Black Sands Beach Turtle watching
- Daily swimming, cycling and running
- Active volcano lava tour
- Coffee plantation tour

Four Former World Champions - sharing race tips

Race Morning

The bike racks and transition on the pier were immaculate. Every inch was carpeted and nothing was out of place. It was not cramped for space, like in ordinary races. This event was clearly going to be different from all the others. There was terrific kind attention from the army of volunteers and marshals. The excitement and expectation was palpable.

The sunrise was sensational as we did the final bike check then waded into the water for the start. I had seen this iconic race start on TV, DVD's and on Youtube many times. It seemed unreal and yet very familiar.

The mass start at Dig-Me Beach and the cannon going off were wonderful. It felt like 'home', despite being almost as different from a UK triathlon start as it is possible to be. I felt no particular stress or worries about that swim in that lovely clear warm tropical calm water. There was nothing for me to prove to anybody on the swim. However, there was slight anxiety that any number of bike issues could spoil this, possibly once in a lifetime, experience.

Swim

Sensibly I seeded myself with the slowest 10%, far to the left of the pier. The beautiful warm clear water had lots of fish to keep us company. I had gazed at the sea-life and sighted the tropical landscape every morning for the last week, but on race day it was the same pair of feet of the swimmer in front to look at for most of the 1:27 swim. It was a massive non-wetsuit swim PB for me but one of the slowest swims of the day in this elite field (2100th out of 2316).

The swimming was all serene until the final half-mile when the top female age-groupers, who had set off 15 mins later than the men, bombed past and over me.

Cycle

There was no problem finding my bike bag or bike in Transition as the bulk of my age group were long gone.

There are some slightly tricky sections at mile 2 and mile 4.5, so I took it easy and settled down. This cycle must not be ruined by a stupid accident.

The plan was to drink 1500ml per hour (yes, 1500ml!) and not get in an accident or get a drafting penalty. It seemed almost impossible to drink that much but experts say it is needed at Kona. The heat, high winds and humidity readily cause dehydration plus salt depletion. Feed stations every 7 miles were needed in order to get enough to drink and to constantly drench the body in water. One bike bottle-cage was used just to hold water for body-drenching in between feed stations.

There appeared to be double the usual number of draft-buster motorbike marshals and the penalty tents were always full.

A rushed 4 minute T1 caused insufficient suncream application, so the subsequent fear of sunburn encouraged quicker pedalling.

The gusts of wind in the northern half of the bike course were extreme and it was good to not have deep wheel rims (Zipp 303 front and 808 rear did the job nicely).

Good pacing was achieved using a heart rate monitor and I overtook lots of people in the last 30 miles. The 5:55 cycle was pleasing and the DIY bike constructed from eBay second-hand parts performed perfectly.

Run

It was a massive relief to start the run and feel confident that this most important of all races would now be completed. Running is 'my time to shine'.

Extreme overheating potential was mitigated by feed stations every mile issuing fluids, sponges, gels and ice. It was good having the drink bottle carried in the tri-suit back pocket to provide extra drinks in between each feed station.

Lots of ice was stuffed under tri-suit and hat but it mostly melted within 10 minutes. Many supporters on the course had water hoses to cool us. Athletes who overheated had to slow down but fortunately, I kept a good pace even in the infamous hot microclimate of the 4-mile "natural energy lab" section.

It was great feeling strong during the hot airless ascent out of the 'energy lab' (just before mile 20) and thereafter gradually increasing pace to overtake many athletes until completing the run in 3:53. The final half-mile mile was an ecstatic sprint ending in a mad dash to the finisher's arch. I was too pumped-up with emotion to slow-down and pose for pictures.

Helen was a volunteer marshall for the finish-line and I literally ran into her arms, which was a very special moment to complete a wonderful event.

Dr Graham completes Ironman in Hawaii

Triathlon

Drs James and Helen Graham from Hassocks have been to Hawaii for the World Ironman Championships, which Jim competed in on Sunday.

The Championships included additional warm up events, so Helen was also able to take part with Jim in a 10km run on Monday, in which she came second in her age group, winning a medal and mug.

They both also did a 3.8km swim race with Jim finishing in 1.35 and Helen in 1.55. Following this there was a traditional Hawaiian feast.

The Ironman event took place on Sunday and James said: "I gave it my all and had a good race. It looks like I may be in the top half of my category, which is very pleasing,

considering these athletes are the best of the best. It was incredibly hot and very windy at times on the bike.

"I drank countless litres of fluid and constantly drenched myself in water to keep cool. I

"Ice was distributed all over my body under my tri suit and hat. I lost count of the salt tablets taken. I got sunburn despite sunscreen. But it was an unforgettable experience."

Helen then did the 'Following Morning Sprint Triathlon' on Monday. She said it was an enjoyable low key event, but it did attract one professional Rachael Mcbride, who was lovely. Helen, normally a longer distance runner, said the run was too short for her catch the opposition, but she is pleased to have the tee shirt.

Dr James Graham with his medal

Race Summary
Swim
01:27:49 (Division Rank: 185 at end of swim)
Bike
05:55:52 (Division Rank: 150 at end of cycle)
Run
03:53:34 (Division Rank: 101 at end of marathon)
Transition Details
T1: Swim-to-bike 00:04:35
T2: Bike-to-run 00:04:52

Finish Time
11:26:42
Overall Rank 1,316 out of 2,316
Division Rank (age 50-54) 101 out of 203

Post-Race

The next day was spent 'chilling out', packing the bikes and attending the Champions Banquet Awards Ceremony.

A couple of days after the big race we found ourselves jogging for miles in the lava fields to get access to the latest up-close viewing places. Big Island Hawaii is literally still growing, with huge quantities of red-hot lava being deposited on land and at sea every day. At sunset the bubbling lava glows spectacularly and it looks like the end of the world and the beginning of the world simultaneously.

Reflection and Thanks

This is the race report that I have dreamed about writing since first doing a local sprint triathlon in 2008. Some people apparently have sufficient ability to get a Kona slot at will. For most of us it is nearly impossible and that makes this achievement sweeter. My journey has been blessed with plenty of help and support from family and friends.

Being placed 101st out of 203 starters in the 50-54 male age group was almost unbelievable. Going by qualifying race results, I should have been one of the slowest in the age group. I would have been content to beat just one of them in order to prove that my participation in the World Championship was justified.

Mid Sussex Triathlon Club is full of so many inspirational people who provide lots of positive energy and all of our successes should be considered a team effort. It was fantastic for me to share this experience with my most important person (Helen).

THE END

Bill Capps
1935 to 2017

23271219R00144

Printed in Great Britain
by Amazon